Meritocracy and Americans' Views on Distributive Justice

Meritocracy and Americans' Views on Distributive Justice

RICHARD T. LONGORIA

LEXINGTON BOOKS

A division of
ROWMAN & LITTLEFIELD PUBLISHERS, INC.
Lanham • Boulder • New York • Toronto • Plymouth, UK

LEXINGTON BOOKS

A division of Rowman & Littlefield Publishers, Inc.
A wholly owned subsidiary of The Rowman & Littlefield Publishing Group, Inc.
4501 Forbes Boulevard, Suite 200
Lanham, MD 20706

Estover Road
Plymouth PL6 7PY
United Kingdom

British Library Cataloguing in Publication Information Available

Library of Congress Cataloging-in-Publication Data

Longoria, Richard T., 1977–
Meritocracy and Americans' views on distributive justice / Richard T. Longoria.
p. cm.
Includes bibliographical references and index.
ISBN-13: 978-0-7391-2348-5 (cloth: alk. paper)
ISBN-10: 0-7391-2348-3 (cloth: alk. paper)
ISBN-13: 978-0-7391-3222-7 (electronic: alk. paper)
ISBN-10: 0-7391-3222-9 (electronic: alk. paper)
1. Elite (Social sciences)—United States. 2. Equality—United States. 3. Merit (Ethics)—United States. 4. Social status—United States. 5. Justice—United States—Public opinion. 6. Public opinion—United States. I. Title.
HN90.E4L67 2009
305.5'13—dc22

2008033477

Printed in the United States of America

™ The paper used in this publication meets the minimum requirements of American National Standard for Information Sciences—Permanence of Paper for Printed Library Materials, ANSI/NISO Z39.48–1992.

To my mother, Blanca. This wouldn't have been possible without you.

Contents

List of Tables

Preface

This project stems from a long-standing fascination with the idea of meritocracy. In theory a meritocratic society is one in which every person is given an equal opportunity to succeed and where one's race, gender, social background, personal connections, and other irrelevant characteristics have no effect on one's outcome in life. Instead, only a person's choices, hard work, and abilities determine their place in society. Meritocracy is an ideal. It's an ideal that we have not yet achieved in America, and perhaps wish not to achieve, but there is a growing public discussion on the matter. This project asks questions that will give us a glimpse into public opinion on the issues of meritocracy.

Previous research has found broad public support for the idea that smart, hardworking people should be rewarded. Why then don't we actually live in a meritocracy? In part this is explained by the finding that most Americans believe that the US is already a meritocracy. That being the case, no special effort is required to achieve the ideal. Another reason is that Americans also display a commitment to values that are resolutely unmeritocratic. Support for individual property rights and the institution of inheritance suggests that most Americans believe that it is just for economic wealth to be distributed by heredity instead of merit. It also finds that many Americans may be skeptical of the idea that the US is already a meritocracy. Race, gender, social background, personal connections and other non-merit factors are believed by many Americans to impact a person's outcome in life. In short, most Americans know that the US has not yet achieved the meritocratic ideal. These contradictory sentiments are probably quite common and explained by deep-seeded value conflicts on issues of distributive justice.

Acknowledgments

Special thanks must be given to the faculty and staff of the University of Maryland, College Park. Its library and online research tools were essential to the collection of data that was used for this project. Faculty from the departments of Government and Politics, Philosophy, and the School of Public Policy assisted in this project by reading early drafts and providing astute commentary. The author would like to thank Mark Graber, Frances Lee, Judith Lichtenberg, Irwin Morris, the late Linda Williams, and most especially James Gimpel for their patience and timely reading of works in progress. This project could not have moved forward without their highly discerning minds and helpfulness to a young scholar. Ileen Bryer at National-Louis University assisted with the index.

None of this would have been possible without the support of my friends and family. Myonnie Bada and other graduate students at the University of Maryland provided sympathetic ears at the informal "pub nights," where discussions ranged from Greek classics, survey methodology, and comprehensive exams to relationships, car problems, and movies. My lifelong buddy Luis Gonzalez provided a break from academia and was always ready to go to a White Sox game on my trips back home to Chicago. My aunts and uncle, Maria, Martha, and Richard, provided financial and moral support during my eleven years of college and graduate school. My mother, Blanca, always encouraged me to continue my studies and sacrificed a great deal to assist me in all my endeavors. It is to her that this book is dedicated.

Chapter 1

What is Meritocracy?

To those of you who received honors, awards,
and distinctions, I say, well done. And to the C students,
I say you too can be president of the United States.[1]

George W. Bush

In this statement at Yale's commencement address, the President, who graduated from Yale, was making a mockery of the idea that merit leads to success. When we typically think of merit, we often associate talent with the particular trait of intelligence and academic prowess. George W. Bush was effectively disassociating political power from the narrow skills associated with book learning. The American republic, it seems, is not the Republic of Plato, which is led by philosopher-kings, nor is it living up to the ideals of Jefferson's "natural aristocracy."

We can all recall that student who was referred to as the "teacher's pet"; some of the readers might even have been that student. But for the most part the other students are likely to recall feelings of animosity, hostility, envy, and sometimes wonder at the student who seemed to so easily grasp new concepts and so easily recalled everything that we were told to read the night before. We especially recall being told that that person was the kind of person that was going to be successful. Through brainpower and hard work, that person was destined to have a higher status than all of us for the rest of our lives. Did it actually work out that way?

George W. Bush's success is based on an entirely different set of characteristics than those of pure merit. His grandfather was a wealthy financier, US Senator from Connecticut, and Yale graduate. His father was a US Congressman, CIA director, Vice President, and later President of the United States. His father also graduated from Yale and would come to marry Barbara Pierce Bush. She was the granddaughter of an Ohio Supreme Court Justice and a descendent of Franklin Pierce, the 14th president of the United States (McNamee & Miller 2004, 84). George W. Bush's power seems to emanate from a political dynasty that is based on hereditary privilege.

This type of hereditary privilege, while entirely contradictory to the principles of meritocracy, is in fact a fairly common occurrence in America and one that is based on a different set of values. Richard J. Daley, the longtime machine boss and mayor of Chicago, was once accused of providing special privileges to his children. His son was awarded a lucrative city contract for insurance services and local reporters viewed this as evidence of corruption and patronage. The mayor, far from denying the charges, stated, "It's a father's duty to help his sons" (Clark 2000, 18). Helping one's child is not a crime; it is a responsibility. And what is more, helping one's offspring is not immoral, it is what makes one an honorable man. In many cities the Mayor's statement would have caused public outrage, but in Chicago the public nodded their heads in approval of their honorable mayor and patriarch.[2] Eventually, they would elect his son, Richard M. Daley, to be mayor and, as Chicagoans often joke, the children of the city would come to believe that the Daley clan had the unusual habit of naming their boys "Mayor." It was simply a fact of life and not one that was cause for concern. Things were exactly as they should be.

This state of affairs would no doubt horrify the founders of the American Republic. Their vision of an ideal nation seems not to have filtered down to the masses. The founders struggled in a revolutionary battle to usurp monarchy and the hereditary transmission of political power. When Thomas Paine vehemently argued for independence in *Common Sense* he said,

> To the evil of monarchy we have added that of hereditary succession.... For all men being originally equals, no *one* by *birth* could have a right to set up his own family in perpetual preference to all others for ever, and though himself might deserve *some* decent degree of honors of his contemporaries, yet his descendants might be far too unworthy to inherit them (Paine 1976, 76).

He is claiming that we should properly reward those who we deem meritorious but that this merit cannot be transmitted. Specifically, he goes on to say, "When we are planning for posterity, we ought to remember that virtue is not hereditary" (Paine 1976, 110). If we do not wish to put that statement on par with other "self-evident" truths, we could certainly put it into the category of blatantly obvious to anyone with common sense.

Still, we have a peculiar penchant to accept as legitimate a status claim that is based on aristocratic and feudal notions of desert. As a value we may call it "non-ideological particularism" (Clark 1975, 321). Rather than seeking to apply general rules to particular situations, or what social scientists call "universalism" (Parsons 1937), we evaluate people according to their individual ascriptive traits. Instead of "looking for the best person for the job," which applies a general rule for selection, we may believe that "a person deserves special consideration because he is the son of so and so." Besides our conceptions of desert based on merit, we also draw upon other values irrespective of merit to decide who gets what and who gets treated how.

Privilege based on hereditary claims is a long-standing element of English culture, and though we ostensibly rejected many of those claims, Americans are nevertheless the cultural inheritors of that and other Western values that emanate from our English cultural origins. Students of British history will readily acknowledge that England had "strong class-based cultures, visible from clothing, audible from accent and embodied in mannerisms" (Ambercrombie & Ward, et.

al. 2000, 147). While American society did undergo a great transformation during the battle for independence, we still retained many of our cultural traditions. The difference for Americans is that we were forced to justify our exalting of some over others on different grounds than in the past.

Origins of the Term

The term "meritocracy" was introduced in a social satire written in the 1950s where social goods and positions are distributed solely on the basis of merit. In *The Rise of the Meritocracy*, Michael Young emphasizes two major theoretical conflicts. The first is distributive and focuses on selection by family and selection by merit (Young 1994, 20). According to the theory, inherited position and nepotism are antithetical to distribution by merit. The second conflict is political. Democracy is rule by the people, while meritocracy is rule by the cleverest people (Young 1994, 11). Writing retrospectively as a narrator in the future, he finds himself in a situation where democracy no longer seems appropriate. Democracy, he believes, worked when there wasn't equality of opportunity because the clever members of the lower classes could organize and lead their group (Young 1994, 125). In this way the parliament of the past was full of talented people (Young 1994, 125). But once a meritocracy emerged and equal opportunity was achieved, there was nothing for the lower classes to complain about; they had every possible opportunity to rise above their station and the labor movement collapsed, in part because it lacked leaders.

A close reading of his satire reveals that a meritocracy is an "ideal type" society. Although one would be hard pressed to find any society that completely fits the meritocratic model, one can compare an existing society to the model and determine to what extent it is meritocratic. One can also list the core values behind the promotion of meritocracy and determine whether these values are held by contemporary Americans. The central question addressed in this book is, "Do Americans support meritocracy or do they value unmeritocratic distributive schemes?"

The Means and Ends of Meritocracy

At the core of all theories of justice there is a single question: Who is deserving of what? Meritocracy gives a particular answer to this question, but it is often misunderstood or defined only incompletely. There are generally accepted notions of merit having to do with skills and talents (Fullinwider and Lichtenberg 2004, 25). Presumably, the only just consideration in making a distributive decision should be whether the person has the necessary abilities or has a greater abundance of those abilities than others. This question of desert is addressed by

David Miller, who believes that, "Roughly speaking, when we say that a person deserves some benefit on the basis of a quality, we are anticipating a future performance in which that quality is displayed.... If a judgment of merit cannot be linked in this way to an anticipated performance, then we do not have desert in its proper meaning" (Miller 1999, 137). While this commonsense understanding of merit as "the ability to do the job" makes sense, it is limited because it does not consider a person's opportunities for acquiring the skills to do the job.

An often-overlooked theme in Young's book lies at the very foundation of the social theory. There is no meritocracy prior to the establishment of equal opportunity. This should act as a precondition to any discussion of meritocracy. As long as the family and class background have an influence on a person's outcome, the distribution of social goods are not distributed entirely on merit. In its ideal, it is only after these factors are eliminated that the distribution of goods and positions can be based on merit. In short, the correlation between one's social origins and one's outcome in life is zero in a meritocracy. Unfortunately, many people's conception of merit is independent of the opportunities available to others. For these individuals, a person can have merit even if society is actively discriminating against a class of persons on non-merit related grounds. Those people may not fully appreciate the ends of a meritocratic society.

If one of the ends of meritocracy is to provide everyone with an equal opportunity, then what exactly do we mean by "equal opportunity?" In an ideal meritocracy we have a society where every individual, regardless of circumstances of birth, can realistically compete with more advantaged members of society and upward social mobility occurs easily for those who are talented and make use of their talents. This is the basis for the meritocrat's definition of equal opportunity. Based on the end that is sought, the minimum set of opportunities distributed to all in a meritocracy is very high indeed, but it is not infinite. The realistic competitiveness discussed here does not mean that the mentally disabled should be made to compete with the child prodigy. It only means that persons of the same innate capacity will not be hampered or assisted by their social origins and will, if they so choose, achieve the same results in society. The only limits on individual achievements in a meritocracy are natural ability, effort, and individual choices. This requires that the minimum level of resource allocations to the disadvantaged be quite great, but not limitless.

Young's idealized meritocracy is a society that strives for other ends as well. It strives to improve efficiency and international competitiveness by maximizing human potential in the country (Young 1994, 4, 21, 85) and to increase upward and downward social mobility (Young 1994, 5, 43, 60). Although not a central part of the theory, improving efficiency and international competitiveness serves as a legitimizing claim for the more important elements. For some, "distributive justice can be realized only to the extent that each person has complete, and equal opportunity to develop fully his or her *potential* for productivity" (Haslett 1997, 138). This is because limiting an individual's ability to fully develop their natural talents creates social and economic loss in the form of less able social and economic actors. If Bill Gates' family had been too poor to buy him his first computer and there was no social safety net to provide him with one, then Gates and everyone in society loses out. Our production of human capital operates below maximum efficiency when some members of society are denied the opportunity to acquire skills and training. In effect, we would be producing sub-optimal human resources. The provision of resources works to improve the chances of upward mobility for smart, hard-working individuals.

These ends are accomplished through specific means that are carried out through public policy. Civil service exams eliminate nepotism and seniority and choose among applicants through tests that measure merit (Young 1994, 9, 69, 78). The theory, as formulated by Young, also proposes paying clever children allowances so that they will stay in school (Young 1994, 48) and that universities select among applicants through objective examinations that measure merit (Young 1994, 50). In this ideal society, the influence of the family is weakened and the role of the school is enhanced (Young 1994, 30) through Goffman-like total institutions that substitute kinship so that children don't spend their spare time with their family, which may have a "lower culture" (Young 1994, 59). In theory, boarding schools become the mechanism by which lower class children are socialized into the upper class world they are moving to.

Research shows that wealthy individuals use boarding schools to provide their own children with the cultural capital necessary to succeed. This is done by weakening the family bond and preparing their children for a place among the elite (Cookson & Persell 1985). Meritocratic theory supposes that boarding schools can have a similar effect on disadvantaged youths and in the ideal are used along with the traditional day school. This particular idea, however, is not new to those interested in education. Lipset notes that the Workingmen's Party of the 1820s advocated state financed boarding schools for the common child because class-based cultural advantages could not be eliminated without such extraordinary effort (Lipset 1996, 82). Indeed, the notion of remolding the young to fit society's ends is an idea that has been thought about since the classical era.

Finally, and perhaps most importantly, the theory seeks the elimination of the inheritance of property because it rewards those who may lack merit with unearned wealth (Young 1994, 26). Nepotism, or the assistance of one's own child over the children of others, may be a biological impulse (Bellow 2003, 22), but it is in direct conflict with the meritocratic ideal. Meritocracy is an individual-regarding distributive theory, not a group-regarding theory. Individuals who display superb ability and effort deserve rewards; it is not the groups they belong to that deserve the rewards. Hence it is not legitimate in a meritocracy to reward a person's family, ethnic/racial group, city, or nation for the achievements of the individual. Although these groups may benefit from the achievements of a person in their group, they would not be the direct recipients of any reward due to the individual nor would they be entitled to the reward by proxy of the individual.

Characteristics that are inherited from the parent such as race, ethnicity, class, and social status cannot have a bearing on the child's success in a meritocracy. When rewarding a meritorious parent, the meritocracy cannot go so far as to destroy meritocracy for future generations. Wealth for the parent, though merited, is not allowed to destroy the very system it sought to establish. It is a system where people are judged and rewarded for having relevant personal characteristics that are independent of characteristics of the parent. The argument that "my ancestors earned it" is not a legitimate reason for a descendent to lay claim on wealth and other advantages. They must compete for rewards based on their own merit just as any other individual must. It is through all these various policies that the meritocratic ideal is turned into a reality. For some it is also the manner in which social justice is attained.

To summarize, a meritocratic society is one that promotes smart, hard-working individuals regardless of which social strata they happen to be born in. It is a society where one's race, gender, and social background does not influence their outcome and where every individual, regardless of circumstances of birth, can realistically compete with more advantaged members of society. It is a society where equality of opportunity is a reality and where the restraints on individual success (except for innate capability) are eliminated as far as is possible. The items that are necessary to provide individuals with an equal opportunity to succeed in society are not distributed by merit, but are provided to all on an equal basis. Inherited position and nepotism are eliminated in a meritocratic society.

Commonsense Ideas about Meritocracy

The most basic understanding of meritocratic distribution is that the distributed social good not be distributed by heredity or any other characteristic unrelated to performance. Those that are the most able to perform the task, or who have demonstrated the highest ability, should receive the reward. Here, people argue that the person with the best qualifications should get the reward and the qualifications are limited to the abilities that are necessary for the performance of designated tasks. A person's connections or family ties are not directly related to the ability to perform, therefore, the Economist writes, "The United States likes to think of itself as the very embodiment of meritocracy: a country where people are judged on their individual abilities rather than their family connections" ("Ever higher society"). One's performance, not family connections, is the basis for most people's understanding of merit as a distributive rule.

But merit may also be about having the "right stuff." And the "right stuff" consists of "being talented, having the right attitude, working hard, and having a high moral character" (McNamee & Miller 2004, 21). This commonsense notion harkens back to Jefferson's "virtue and talent" of the natural aristocracy, but at its heart it is still about upward mobility and deserving one's outcome in life. According to McNamee and Miller,

> America is seen as the land of opportunity where people get out of the system what they put into it. Ostensibly, the most talented hardest working, and most virtuous get ahead. The lazy, shiftless, and indolent fall behind. You may not be held responsible for where you start out in life, but you are responsible for where you end up. If you are truly meritorious, you will overcome any obstacle and succeed (McNamee & Miller 2004, 3).

Given that different notions of "virtue" have prompted philosophers to write volumes on the matter, it is unlikely (and very difficult) to determine just what the public might expect from a "virtuous" leader. Merit, while still complicated, is more straightforward. It's about one's performance. And one's performance is measured by one's ability and effort.

For the sake of clarity, we may wish to call this idea of merit "technical merit." It is limited to a person's demonstrated ability or expectations about future performance at given tasks. When selecting an employee by technical merit, the employer must choose the person, or among the persons, who have the ability, selecting the employee with the most ability, if there is such a candidate. Technical merit is not influenced by the initial set of opportunities available to different individuals. It is a measure of raw ability, regardless of others' opportunity to acquire the ability. Therefore a person could claim to merit a reward because of his/her superior abilities, even if other individuals are actively denied any opportunity to develop their own talents and skills.

One need not stretch their imagination too far to conceive of a situation where members of one racial group are actively prohibited from educational opportunities and forced into the lower paid workforce because of inadequate skills. The favored racial group, with a monopoly on important educational resources, receives the training that allows its individual members to acquire the skills to perform tasks that command higher salaries. Because individuals in the favored group possess the necessary skills and talents, while individuals in the disfavored group do not, the individuals in the favored group claim to have more merit than individuals in the disfavored group. Questions of distributive justice are therefore a central element in most discussions of merit.

Outline of the Book

This book is about what the American public believes is just. Specifically, it is about the extent to which Americans support or reject the ideal of meritocracy. It begins in chapter 2 with an overview of the uses and limits of public opinion research. Often public opinion seems mercurial and irrational. This is because the public is largely uninformed about political issues and holds contradictory values. When one value is emphasized over another value, different responses can be elicited for the same question. This does not mean that public opinion is useless; it only means that public opinion is limited to understanding which values are made salient when specific questions or problems are raised. Understanding these values brings us closer to understanding American society.

These conflicting values, however, can be put into context by understanding the theoretical and philosophical debate over meritocracy. Some theorists believe that meritocracy is unjust because they value non-arbitrary distributive schemes, the integrity of the family, social mobility, the free market, cost effective or efficient government policies, and democracy. Others support meritocracy because they value rewards being distributed by effort and ability, individual autonomy, equal opportunity, social mobility, competition, and rule by the best. Often these values come into direct conflict with each other or can be made to support and oppose the same policies. Nevertheless, the philosophical debate can frame public opinion by pointing us towards potential problems with the meritocratic ideal.

Chapter 3 offers readers a glimpse into the conflict by presenting evidence of majority support and opposition to meritocracy. Most Americans believe that hard work and intelligence should be rewarded, but they also value using non-merit criteria for the distribution of social goods. Many Americans believe anyone can achieve success if they are willing to work hard, but they also know that race, gender, and social background can influence one's outcome in life. African Americans and whites have much in common when it comes to their idea of the good society; both groups believe that everyone should be given an equal opportunity to succeed. The difference is that most whites view the world as a meritocracy where everyone can succeed, while African Americans are less certain of that prospect.

In the specific case of inheritance taxation, chapter 4 finds that Americans flatly reject the meritocratic ethos. After a discussion of the history of inheritance, it finds that the distribution of wealth along hereditary lines is accepted by most Americans. This is in direct contradiction to the proposition that everyone should work for their money. There is support for the reduction or elimination of the estate tax that most likely stems from a generalized anti-tax sentiment, unrealistic optimism, and sympathy for small business owners and farmers. However, the estate tax issue is a very low priority for most Americans. This is not surprising given that so few are affected by it. Most Americans would prefer a reduction in the taxes that actually affect them, such as the income or fuel tax, rather than a reduction of the estate tax. When Americans are told that the estate tax pays for social security and education programs, public opinion supports the tax. In this way framing has a significant impact on majority opinion on the issue.

Chapter 5 begins by providing readers with a short history of affirmative action policy in the US, from the 1960s civil rights struggles to the lawsuits over college admissions in 2003. It then gives an overview of the debate over the justness of the policy. Most Americans believe that discrimination is not very prevalent and this is the key to understanding differences of opinion about affirmative action. Most African Americans don't support race-based preferences that discriminate against whites, but they do tend to believe that racial preferences are needed to correct injustice and to provide a level playing field for all. Both the supporters and opponents of affirmative action use meritocratic values to make their case. Opponents argue that merit alone should decide who gets selected for promotions or college admissions, while supporters argue that society should do everything it can to give people an opportunity to acquire the skills and assets that would allow them to overcome discrimination.

What does all of this mean for democracy? Chapter 6 begins with a brief history of mass behavior that shows the reader how groups can be irrational and violent even when each of the group's members is not. For that reason, democratic theory has often been defensive about the role that "the people" should play in a democratic polis. The result is an American constitutional system that places a check on the power of the people. In today's world we now have methods to collect and aggregate individual preferences. But can public opinion polls actually serve as a measure of the "will of the people," especially when "the people" seem ignorant, volatile, and contradictory? The rise of value pluralism in political theory poses a new problem for those who study society. While it may be good to allow different values to be expressed, contradictory values produce illogical and irrational preferences. Therefore, relying on "core values" to guide government is extremely problematic.

The final chapter summarizes the findings of the project. Public opinion on questions of meritocracy is contradictory. But this is no reason to ignore or dismiss public opinion. With an understanding of where the conflict lies, educators can ask students the difficult questions and political leaders can prepare for difficult choices.

Notes

1. quoted in McNamee & Miller 2004, 95

2. If one thinks this is a historical fluke, it should be noted that on July 18, 2006, Todd Stroger was selected by party leaders to replace his father, incumbent John Stroger, on the ballot for Cook County Board President after his father suffered a stroke. On November 7, 2006, he was elected despite protestations of nepotism by his challenger. On August 21, 2008, Illinois Senate President Emil Jones announced that he would like his son to take his seat when he retires. Other Illinois politicians with political parents include Illinois Attorney General Lisa Madigan, Illinois Comptroller Dan Hynes, U.S. Congressman Jesse Jackson Jr., and U.S. Congressman Daniel Lipinski.

Chapter 2

Understanding Public Opinion and the Philosophical Debate

The public must be put in its place, so that it may exercise its own powers, but no less and perhaps even more, so that each of us may live free of the trampling and the roar of the bewildered herd.[1]

Walter Lippmann

Many people who study public opinion believe that the public is ill-informed and mercurial in their attitudes. The general will, if it can exist at all, is not a well-reasoned conviction but a passing response to a fleeting question. For this reason, and others, the public lacks a single decisive voice. They vacillate from one response to another depending on the manner the question is asked or on the ordering of the questions. They sometimes support and sometimes oppose the same policy and they often vacillate between liberal and conservative views.

As a college instructor, I sometimes ask undergraduates in my political science courses if they believe that "people should work for their money." The overwhelming majority agree with that proposition as nearly every person in the room raises their hand. I then ask, "Do you think that wealthy people should be allowed to pass on their money to their children?" Again an overwhelming majority believes that wealthy individuals are entitled pass on their wealth to family members. I then ask, "So the child of the wealthy person doesn't have to work for their money, is that right?" Looks of confusion appear, students look at each other and most then begin to retract one or the other statement. One particularly bright student once raised his hand and exclaimed, "If we think that smart, hard-working people should have more money than others, then we can't also have a system that gives money to people who haven't demonstrated that they're smart or hard-working. We can't have meritocracy *and* inheritances." Students who were purportedly the beneficiaries of large estates reacted passionately against the implications of that statement. But the point, that most were unaware of the conflict, was made, and people had to come to terms with their cognitive dissonance.

The students I've encountered do not have a sophisticated distributive justice schema that justifies both earned income and inherited wealth. For most, if not all, of the students, it may have been the first time in their lives that the two questions were asked consecutively. It's as though at that moment the clouds part, a ray of sunshine hits them in the face, and a truth is revealed to them. I like to believe that my introduction to political science brings them one step closer to personal enlightenment. They become aware of the internal conflict of values that most Americans share.

Unfortunately, many Americans never experience this type of educating moment. They remain ignorant and give contradictory, confused, and seemingly haphazard answers to questions. Intellectuals and civic leaders, however, are supposed to be wiser. They should have consistent views based on well-reasoned arguments and empirical evidence. But often these very smart individuals disagree with each other, especially when it comes to the notion of meritocracy. Philosophers, sociologists, and political scientists have all contributed to a new discourse about the goals and ideals of human society. Some of them support meritocracy, but many oppose it. It is therefore appropriate to provide the reader with an overview of the intellectual debate on the issue of meritocracy.

This chapter seeks to accomplish two things. First, it will explain why Americans give contradictory answers to questions. It will discuss how opinions are formed and consider the uses and limits of polling generally and of the methods employed in this project specifically. Second, it will provide an overview of the many important issues raised in the philosophical debates about meritocracy. The chapter serves as a lens that the reader can use to understand the public opinion data that is presented in subsequent chapters. It also takes the relatively straightforward concept of meritocracy that was developed in chapter 1 and addresses some of the more nuanced elements of the ideal.

They Don't Know What's Good for Them

One of the most enduring findings in public opinion literature is that there is a great deal of inconsistency in people's responses to questions. Converse finds that individuals do not have very stable preferences over time. He shows that the masses have low levels of ideological constraint, often vacillating between liberal and conservative views, and that their positions are unstable or even randomly formulated (Converse 1964). He goes so far as to say that the public's attitudes are actually "non-attitudes" (Converse 1970).

This is in large part due to the public's general inattentiveness to politics. The public, it seems, is ignorant when it comes to basic information about politics. Most Americans are simply not informed about most of the issues most of the time. In studies, only 29% of Americans could name their Congressional representative, only 25% could name the two US Senators from their home state (Glynn et. al. 1999, 23), and only 9% could correctly name the Chief Justice of the Supreme Court (Barnum 1993, 215). Indeed, "more than two-thirds could not name a single member of the Court" (Barnum 1993, 215 [ft 8]). These data show that citizens know very little about the people who make decisions on their behalf.

Other studies have concluded that Americans know next to nothing about the performance of parties or individual office holders (Miller & Stokes 1962). Even those who claim to know an incumbent's position on issues are very often wrong (Hurley & Hill 1980). This could be because the public is simply too busy to be aware of all that occurs in government (Lippmann 1993, 15; Lippmann 1997, 37). But regardless of the reasons, a lack of information can cause a respondent to answer "incorrectly." According to a recent study,

> People who are well informed about politics are better able to form opinions consistent with their political predispositions, which means that opinion givers who are ill informed may be mistaken about their needs, wants, and values: they might give opinions that they wouldn't give if they were more knowledgeable about politics (Althaus 2003, 148).

The lack of information can even cause an individual to support a party that opposes that person's stated attitudes and policy preferences (Campbell, et. al. 1964, 120). This would be like an anti-war pacifist voting for a pro-war candidate because he didn't know which candidate was more hawkish. A fully informed public is likely to give different answers to various questions than the poorly informed public that exists.

Because of these low levels of information many people are easily swayed during political or economic crisis (Campbell, et. al. 1964, 284). Individuals with high levels of political information are usually the most involved in politics and have created a "perceptual screen" to filter out or dismiss information that is contrary to their view. For these individuals the new information does not affect their opinion. Those with low levels of information lack the "perceptual screens" and accept the new information often resulting in a switch of sentiment on the issue (Campbell, et. al. 1964, 75).

Studies continue to show that media coverage is particularly influential on those that are the least involved in politics (Zaller 1992, 13). Those who are more politically engaged are less influenced by television news coverage because of their greater capacity to screen out contradictory evidence or to recall an opposing consideration when confronted with unfavorable facts. The uninvolved accept and internalize transmitted ideas with less hesitation and are therefore easily manipulated by media coverage. This results in the transitory and unstable positions that are commonly found among the least informed individuals.

Give the Public a Chance; They Are Rational

On the other side of the coin there are those who believe that public opinion is rational. They believe that the problems outlined above can be remedied. The first solution to the problem of uninformed opinion-giving is to do nothing at all. If the uniformed public is answering questions as though they were flipping a coin, then "for" and "against" responses will cancel each other out. Meanwhile, if the informed public consistently gives one answer over another, then majority opinion will reflect the opinions of the most informed respondents.

Two problems with this approach are readily apparent. First, if the uninformed public tends to give one answer over another, they can effectively "drown out" the opinion of informed respondents. Secondly, since the most informed response-givers tend to be better educated, wealthier, middle aged, have professional occupations, and are more likely to be white, then the responses of the most informed opinion givers will be biased toward particular policy preferences that reflect their more elite status (Althaus 2003, 17).

Another approach is to include filter questions that remove uninformed respondents. By asking respondents, "Have you thought about the following issue recently . . ." or "Do you have an opinion on . . ." a researcher could remove respondents who are admittedly uninformed or have no opinion. In this way the respondent is not forced to make up an answer to a question he has never before considered. But again, removing many of these "don't know" respondents may tend to disproportionately remove respondents from lower socio-economic groups.

Perhaps the most influential method of overcoming response instability is the method created by Page and Shapiro, who aggregate responses to the same question over time. Despite the fact that individuals may give different responses to the same questions in different iterations of the survey, "over a period of time, each individual will have a central tendency of opinion, which might be called the 'true' or *long-term preference*, and which can be ascertained by averaging the opinions expressed by the same individual at several different times" (Page & Shapiro 1992, 16). Relying on the classic "canceling out" argument, they state, "simple statistical reasoning indicates that those errors will tend to cancel each other out when the opinions of individuals are aggregated" and "the logic of averaging out random fluctuations in order to find a stable central tendency applies even better to *collective* than to individual opinion" (Page & Shapiro 1992, 20).

The process of aggregating public opinion was a statistical breakthrough, but is subject to many of the same critiques cited above. There is evidence to suggest that ill-informed respondents are sometimes "lop-sided" in their responses. That is, "individual-level information effects tend to occur in systematic rather than random directions. Aggregation alone cannot redeem an ill-informed public" (Althaus 2003, 122). Even though there are methodological techniques that attempt to mitigate the effects of an ill-informed public, we have yet to develop a foolproof method for collecting opinions in a manner that yields "enlightened preferences" or the "general will."

Clues to Opinion Formation

Being ill-informed is only the beginning of the problem. Researchers know why responses are unstable, but the reader may also be interested in how the contradictions manifest themselves. Because of their lack of information those responding to survey questions tend to provide answers from the "top of the head" (Lockerbie & Borrelli 1990, 196; Zaller 1992, 33). The instability occurs because some considerations become more salient than others and are more easily recalled when confronted with an unexpected survey question. Similarly, the question and the questions preceding it may raise the saliency of some considerations over others and thus increase the probability of particular responses even though the respondent had no firm position one way or another (Bishop, et. al. 1978; Lockerbie & Borrelli 1990; Rasinski 1989; Zaller 1992).

For example, in the 1970s Americans were asked if they would be willing to allow Communist reporters in America and only 37% of respondents agreed that they should be admitted into the country. In the same survey a different random sample was first asked if they favored American reporters being allowed in Russia and the number that favored Communist reporters in America jumped to 73%. This was because most Americans favored American reporters in Russia, which then triggered considerations of reciprocity (Zaller 1992, 32). For Zaller, neither response represents a "true preference" (Zaller 1992, 35). Rather, the first example triggered anti-communist sentiment and the second triggered values of freedom of the press and equality. Americans had and have strong feelings for all these considerations; the difference is that some considerations became more salient at the instant of being asked.

Often these considerations lead Americans to both favor and oppose the same policy (Zaller 1992, 59). A person may support a program to "stop the spread of Communism" when asked about foreign policy, but not support "aid to the Contras" if they are concerned about budget deficits and don't know that the Contras are anti-Communist rebels (Lockerbie & Borrelli 1990, 200; Zaller 1992, 83). Relying on "core values" doesn't lead to a stable attitude. This is because values themselves are transitory; they depend on the situation. The question wording has an effect precisely because Americans value incompatible items.

This inconsistency becomes especially problematic when issues of justice and fairness are presented. It happens that sometimes,

> People appear as strictly 'Rawlsian' in some situations, while they appear as resolutely 'anti—Rawlsian' in others. They are in some circumstances Kantian

> (that is, they tend to follow principles of universal value), while they are rather in other circumstances utilitarian (that is, they tend to follow their interest and hold principles as valid provided they can consider them as serving their interest) (Boudon 2001, 18).

In one situation, an individual may believe that X is fair, while in a different situation the same individual will believe that X is unfair. Sometimes an individual will make their decision about the justness of X based on what he believes is best for society, while in other cases he bases that decision on his own self-interest. It may even be that he will firmly believe that X is good for society and that Y bad for society, but only if X serves his self-interest and Y opposes it.

The prominent sociologist Max Weber was very much aware of this problem when he wrote about social values:

> In his lecture, *Wissenschaft als Beruf*, Weber has used two influential metaphors 'value polytheism' and 'the war between gods.' They suggest that values can be incompatible with one another, that, in some cases, it is impossible to show that one should choose one value rather than another, that social subjects often cannot justify their axiological choices, that is, explain why they endorse such and such value statements (Boudon 2001, 30).

A person may worship the sun god, or they may worship the rain god. But their decision may depend on the weather.

What becomes clear is that "for the majority of persons on the majority of issues, inconsistencies in their considerations concerning different aspects of a given issue remain unresolved and probably unrecognized" (Zaller 1992, 55). Because of a lack of extensive thought about a matter before them and because they have absorbed both arguments for and against a policy, people often vacillate in the responses to given questions. As a consequence of not becoming aware of dissonant attitudes,

> A person may react angrily to a news report of welfare fraud and then, a few weeks later, become equally distressed over other news reports of impoverished children and homeless families. Thus, people may have one reaction to an issue that would cause them to favor it and another that would cause them to oppose it, but—and here is the heart of the argument—for most people, most of the time, there is no need to reconcile or even to recognize their contradictory reactions to events and issues (Zaller 1992, 93).

A person may transition from one value to another depending on their circumstances or most recent experiences. They may value smaller government and the Protestant work ethic and report to oppose welfare programs. They may also value charity and assistance to the poor, believing it is a moral obligation, and consequently support the same welfare programs they previously opposed. People who value both "smaller government" and "assistance to the poor" may have difficulty with the issue of using government programs to help the poor, sometimes preferring the former and sometimes the latter.

Masses and Elites

The masses are unlikely to possess stable, ideologically consistent preferences because of the conflicting values they support. This means that there are limits to what we can learn from public opinion research. Rather than trying to convince the reader that the poll data presented in this project represents Americans' true opinions about merit and distributive justice, this project only attempts to offer a glimpse into the conflicts that Americans may face when confronted with different choices. The values that are tapped by particular questions will become apparent and we can try to understand to what extent Americans are really committed to meritocratic values.

Individual elites are more likely to have ideologically consistent values, but this does not mean that all elites agree with each other. The remaining sections of this chapter will give an overview of the academic debates occurring on the issue of meritocracy. By understanding the debates, the reader can become cognizant of the different values that are used to support and oppose the ideal of meritocracy. Because meritocracy may superficially seem like a wonderful ideal, it may be best to begin with the critique of meritocracy.

The Attack on Meritocracy

Some in academia have a negative view of meritocracy. This stems, in part, from two different conceptions of meritocracy. The first perspective views the idea as (1) a *system of distributive justice*, while the second view of meritocracy analyzes the concept as (2) a *political system*. Critics that follow the first school of thought make four distinct claims that, in their view, make meritocracy unjust. The criticisms are (a) that distribution by merit is arbitrary and destructive, (b) that it creates a hereditary caste system, (c) that it is incompatible with a market-based economic system, and (d) that it is too costly and harmful. Those who view meritocracy primarily in political terms sometimes argue that meritocracy is undemocratic.

Distributive Justice: Arbitrary and Destructive

Those who view meritocracy as a system of distributive justice are sometimes critical of the idea because they believe it is arbitrary and destructive. They argue that because the distribution of talent in society is arbitrary and undeserved the distribution of social rewards would be unjust in a meritocracy. Arbitrary distribution precludes any possibility of earning the merit that is to be rewarded. They also believe that a "fair opportunity" can't be achieved as long as some form of the family exists in society (Rawls 1971, 64). This is because parents can predispose their children to succeed or fail in life. Parents are a part of the environment that affect the abilities that children attain. Therefore, truly equalizing children's environments in an effort to create a system with equal opportunities for all would mean having to eliminate the family. Under this view, those who believe a person should earn what they have can't support meritocracy because a person can't earn their natural intelligence. People are not responsible for their genetic attributes and are incapable of changing them; therefore, a society that discriminates on the basis of these genetic traits would be unfair. They also support "family values" and are afraid that equal opportunity for all would mean that families can't give their own children a leg up on others.

Distributive Justice: Hereditary Caste System

The second criticism of meritocracy is that it would lead to a hereditary caste system that, far from promoting social mobility, actually makes social advancement nearly impossible for the lower orders. This could be the case if wealth and social position are only, or primarily, distributed by unchangeable genetic characteristics of individuals. If a person's social environment has little or no effect on abilities and outcomes, then public policy changes would not help disadvantaged individuals advance. According to this view, the government could not change the outcomes for individuals unless they engaged in some program of eugenics to change the proportion of certain genes in the population pool. This is, of course, ethically problematic and, at this point, technologically unrealistic. But if true, it would mean that public policy could not affect the distribution of social rewards and it could not affect individuals' social position. The argument has been put into the form of a syllogism:

1. If differences in mental abilities are inherited, and
2. If success requires those abilities, and
3. If earnings and prestige depend on success,
4. Then social standing (which reflects earnings and prestige) will be based to some extent on inherited differences among people (Herrnstein 1971, 197–8)

Compiling evidence from other studies Herrnstein concludes that 80% of the differences in IQ among individuals is explained by inherited factors and 15% is explained by environmental factors (Herrnstein 1971, 171).

These critics believe in a social phenomenon called assortative mating. They found evidence to suggest that people tend to marry others with similar IQ's. They could not discern whether this was because people with similar IQ's are placed close together in school and occupation and are therefore more likely to meet each other, or whether it actually matters in the process of mate selection. Either way, they argue, because IQ is largely inherited, the consequences are enormous because it could lead to a virtual caste system based on intelligence (Herrnstein 1971, 190; Murray & Herrnstein 1994, 110). Young's satire of meritocracy relies on this idea. He believed that eventually discontented meritocrats in his fictional dystopia lead the ignorant masses (they could not organize themselves) to revolt against the upper caste. The inheritability of intelligence would create social instability.

Herrnstein goes on to report some very troubling findings, that, if true, make meritocracy even less pleasant,

> Right from the start the findings were informative. For example, highly bright boys were easier to locate than highly bright girls. And the disparity increased slightly with age, suggesting that whatever I.Q. is, boys maintain it better than girls. . . . In addition, the sample contained an excess of western and northern Europeans and Jews, and shortage of Latins, non-Jewish eastern Europeans, and Negroes (Herrnstein 1971, 129).

Later, he and another author would present more data "proving" that some racial groups score lower than others on measures of intelligence. Herrnstein and Murray suggest that the mean IQ of whites is 101.5, African Americans 85, and East Asians 103. Because they believe that these differences cannot be changed, even if differences in environmental factors are eliminated, they conclude, "For many people, there is nothing they can learn that will repay the cost of the teaching" (Murray & Herrnstein 1994, 520). They not only claim that African Americans are less intelligent than whites, they claim that making expenditures to educate African Americans is a waste of resources.

The implications of this for all disadvantaged groups are devastating because it leads to the type of discrimination that meritocracy seeks to avoid. Individuals who are of low intelligence cannot move up the social ladder in a meritocracy. Those who value social mobility would be forced to oppose meritocracy because meritocracy may ultimately result in a caste system without social mobility.

Distributive Justice: Incompatible with Market

The third argument made against meritocracy is that it conflicts with the ideals of a free market. There is a perceived tension between market distribution and distribution by merit. These critics believe that markets cannot be used to measure merit. They argue that markets reward those who possess something valuable to their fellows, not necessarily rewarding those who fulfill another's conception of merit or desert (Hayek 1944, 135). Furthermore, the market rewards those who have or perform services valued by those with the resources to pay for them. In very important respects, market distribution and distribution by merit lead to different results. Distribution via the market rewards the wealthy while distribution via merit rewards the intelligent and hardworking.

Distributive Justice: Too Costly and Harmful

For some, the notion of equal opportunity for all implies that absolutely everyone should have the same chance to rise above their lot in life. This seems like a great idea until one fully considers the ramifications of the proposal. At first glance, the idea that everyone should have an equal opportunity to succeed seems to imply that the mentally and physically handicapped should be provided with the resources necessary to make them competitive with those who had better circumstances of birth. Clearly, this is not what the theory of meritocracy has in mind. But there are those who define equal opportunity in precisely that way.

The most extreme form of equal opportunity only rewards effort relative to the effort expended by others in the same circumstances (Roemer 1998, 15) and requires the elimination of all inherited differences, including differences in natural ability (Roemer 1998, 23). In this view, equal opportunity can only be achieved at great cost because society would have to compensate those with a lack of natural ability and make them competitive with those who have tremendous natural ability (Roemer 1998, 60–61). In the extreme version, even the disadvantaged may be worse off because of a subsequent decline in the quality of social goods produced. Hypothetically, a few intellectually disadvantaged individuals could be given the resources to train to become surgeons, but because the quality of surgery declines for everyone, even the disadvantaged who don't become surgeons, society loses utility overall (Roemer 1998, 105). In the process of trying to help everyone move up the social ladder, we could actually end up in state where we are all worse off. Simply put, it is more cost effective to train intelligent people than dull people and we are better off as a society when we use our limited resources efficiently. This means abandoning the idea that everyone should have a chance to succeed in life.

Political Justice

From an early age, Americans are taught to believe that democracy is a good thing. But those who view meritocracy as a political system sometimes believe that it is inherently undemocratic. Robert Dahl argues that democracy gives power to the masses while meritocracy alienates power from the masses and gives it to an elite few. His view of meritocracy originates from Plato's guardianship ideal. By guardianship he means, "a regime in which the state is governed by meritorious rulers who consist of a minority of adults, quite likely a very small minority, *and who are not subject to the democratic process*" (Dahl 1989, 57). Those that hold this view are not arguing that experts shouldn't be used by the government, nor that we shouldn't have well educated and virtuous legislators. But they do not believe that those who are deemed to be the most able should govern without check.

Dahl is critical of meritocracy because of five interrelated problems. First, it is difficult to decide what is meant by the necessary "skill, wisdom, and virtue" to lead (Dahl 1967, 19). The characteristics that seem so beneficial to have in a leader may be extraordinarily difficult to define. Second, even if we could decide what is meant by these terms there may be no way to create a system that will actually be able select those who have these characteristics. It could be that the system would be too subjective, or that individuals with malicious intent could game the system and feign the requisite qualities. Third, even if we could devise a system to select the very people we think are best, this does not ensure that they would have the consent of those they are governing. It could happen that the masses don't want to be ruled by those we deem meritorious (Dahl 1967, 20). Fourth, the idea behind attempting to select a small group to rule over others is based on the proposition that the general public does not have the capacity to govern itself wisely or effectively (Dahl 1989, 65). Perhaps we may believe that the masses are ignorant, inconsistent, or mercurial in their preferences. These critics believe that the average citizen has the capacity to act for their own and others' good.

The fifth and most important problem Dahl raises is that even if we could select and approve of rule by the guardians, there is no guarantee that they would remain "skillful, wise, and virtuous" after they are given the authority to rule (Dahl 1967, 20; Dahl 1989, 76). Because he is aware of Lord Acton's aphorism that "absolute power corrupts absolutely," he is suspicious of the ability of even virtuous people to remain that way after they become rulers. He states that, "For anyone convinced by these objections to meritocracy, the main alternative in the United States ever since colonial times has always been popular government" (Dahl 1967, 20). It is clear, then, that some theorists view rule by the meritorious and rule by the people as antagonistic concepts and they believe that the latter is preferred to the former.

Reasons for Optimism

Although I make no claims about being able to overcome these various objections as they stand, some important considerations should be made about their limitations given that the values that are at the root of meritocracy seem to be cherished by many Americans. What we find is that in some cases the values that would lead us reject meritocracy come into direct conflict with other values that would lead us to support it. In other instances, appealing to one's core values is used to provoke unfounded fears about the dangers of meritocracy. And sometimes the same values are used to both support and oppose meritocracy. The meritocratic ideal becomes quite complex when all these considerations are brought to the fore.

Distributive Justice: Arbitrary and Destructive

The first argument held that because the distribution of natural assets is based on "fortune" it is "arbitrary from a moral perspective" (Rawls 1971, 64). Therefore, anything derived from this serendipity is excluded from the concept of justice. Since we can't justify our natural assets, we don't deserve what they bring us. However those that hold this position are sometimes inclined to take the view to its extremes, "Even the willingness to make an effort, to try, and so to be deserving in the ordinary sense is itself dependent on . . . social circumstance" (Rawls 1971, 64). From this we would have to conclude that effort is morally arbitrary as well! A person could no longer be deserving of the products of their efforts.

This argument is dangerous because it belittles people's autonomy. According to Nozick,

> This line of argument can succeed in blocking the introduction of a person's autonomous choices and actions (and their results) only by attributing *everything* noteworthy about the person completely to certain sorts of "external" factors. So denigrating a person's autonomy and prime responsibility for his actions is a risky line to take for a theory that otherwise wishes to buttress the dignity and self-respect of autonomous beings (Nozick 1974, 214).

If everything is arbitrary, a person could no longer be held accountable for their actions because their choices and efforts are considered to be beyond their control. Criminals could not be justifiably penalized because their actions were a result of their environment, not individual volition. Athletes could not deserve trophies because someone else, like parents or coaches, determined the effort the athlete expended at training. And employees could not request a salary in exchange for choosing to work, since they aren't responsible for wanting to be productive and make an effort. In light of admonitions to reward meritorious actions and similar arguments about recognizing personal choices, the first criticism seems to reject any role for individual choices and actions in distributive decisions. Rawls's critique strikes at the heart of the American creed, which values hard work and individual volition. If a person values hard work and believes that hard work should be rewarded, they must reject Rawls's proposition.

The claim that talent is arbitrary is also troubling because talent is a term that can be used to describe both acquired abilities and innate abilities. The latter are what I prefer to call capabilities for the sake of distinguishing between the two concepts. Acquired abilities can be gained through the proper training, but innate capabilities are distributed by chance. Only innate capabilities are subject to Rawls's critique. And, until there is a society where science can control the distribution of particular capabilities through genetics, which does not seem like a particularly appealing idea, there is no manner by which to control the innate capabilities of individuals. Acquired abilities are not distributed randomly and are affected by a variety of social and environmental factors. These can be controlled by society either by allowing for differences in training or by equalizing the amount and type of training. In this way, a good social theorist can discriminate between acquired talents and natural talents and add precision to the confused debate over the role of talent in a meritocracy.

Rawls's second claim is that "fair opportunity" can't be achieved as long as some form of the family exists (Rawls 1971, 64). However, concerns about the institution of the family are not necessarily a reason to preserve the status quo. When family connections and nepotism create unfair advantages for individuals, then it may be legitimate for social action to be taken to compensate for these inequalities. Whether the elimination of inherited wealth is destructive to families is a philosophical debate that is beyond the scope of this particular project, but it is certainly a point of contention among those interested in social justice. A person who values equal opportunity for all children cannot stand for a system that will give advantages to some children while denying them to others.

Distributive Justice: Hereditary Caste System

Upward social mobility for those that are smart and hardworking is at the core of meritocracy. The claim that a meritocratic system of elite recruitment would lead to a genetically based caste system is therefore very troubling. Fortunately, many social scientists have found Herrnstein and Murray's methods problematic and misleading (Fischer 1996; Frasure 1995; Howe 1997; Jencks & Bane 1976). The study that Herrnstein and Murray used to measure IQ differences by race was the Armed Forces Qualifying Test (AFQT), which was given to 12,000 young people in the National Longitudinal Survey of Youth (NLSY). Fischer found that the AFQT did not have a normal distribution in the scores:

> About 20 percent of the test takers answered more than 90 percent of the questions correctly. This is the real distribution of scores from the key measure in *The Bell Curve*. There are simple reasons why the AFQT did not yield a bell curve. Our concern here, however, is with the psychometric insistence that there *must* be a bell curve. The other line in figure 2.1, labeled "Transformed," shows the distribution of test takers after Herrnstein and Murray recalculated

> the scores. It is roughly bell shaped; it is also the source of the title and the jacket design for *The Bell Curve*. How did Herrnstein and Murray get a bell curve from the lopsided distribution of original scores? By a good deal of statistical mashing and stretching. Because they presumed, as psychometricians do, that intelligence must be distributed in a bell curve, they justified transforming the number of questions each test taker correctly answered until they produced the bell curve in the figure (Fischer 1996, 32).

Herrnstein and Murray then focus on the top and bottom 5% of the transformed distribution to show massive inequalities in intelligence that were, in reality, not so far apart.

Contrary to the thesis that genes determine one's intelligence, some psychologists in the field of intelligence testing suggest that IQ is primarily the result of environmental factors. Unfortunately for Herrnstein and Murray's study, the environmental reasons for low IQ were not controlled for and may account for as much as 80% of the difference in scores (Fischer 1996). The pre-natal diet of the mother has been found to have a strong impact on the child's mental capacity throughout life (Broman, Nichols, & Kennedy 1975). The amount of intellectual stimulation that parents can provide a child has the effect of advancing or retarding a child's cognitive development, accounting for a non-genetic passing on of traits. In these situations an environmental factor influences what is perceived to be an innate characteristic.

But even if Herrnstein was correct and intelligence was 80% genetic, the remaining environmental effect could be enormous. There may be "multiplier effects" that could enhance the impact of the environment on individuals. If a small improvement in the environment leads to a small IQ gain and that gain allows one to be in an even more improved environment that leads to even more IQ gains, then, by progression, small environmental differences early in life can have dramatic effects in terms of measured intelligence later on.

> For example, a father who loves basketball and who has a son with slightly better than average genes for the relevant physical traits is likely to play basketball with his son at an early age, and they are likely to play together more often than most. The son may become a bit better at basketball than others his age and may frequently be an early pick when teams are chosen in the school yard. This makes him feel good, so he begins to prefer basketball to other sports. The extra practice makes him better still, and the better he gets, the more he enjoys basketball. He is far more likely than most to be singled out for membership on a school or recreational team where he will receive expert coaching. Such a young person is likely to become a very good basketball player—much better than he would be if his only distinction was the minor physical and social advantages posited at the outset (Dickens & Flynn 2001, 349)

It has been demonstrated that some individuals display large IQ gains over time, a result that cannot occur if IQ was determined at birth (Flynn 1999).

What is more, genes may affect one's environment:

> Imagine a nation that refuses to send children with red hair to school. Under these circumstances, having genes that cause red hair will lower your reading scores. This does not tell us that children with red hair cannot learn to read. It tells only that, in this particular situation, there is a socially imposed relationship between genes and opportunities to learn. In America, the genes that affect skin color have an indirect influence on an individual's opportunities and incentives to learn many skills (Jencks & Bane 1976, 332).

Many people who study the subject find that social class background is related to one's performance on IQ tests. Herrnstein and Murray would argue that is because intelligent couples had intelligent children due to transmitting their genes. But Jencks and others would argue that these children were provided with much better environments early in life and for that reason perform better on exams.

Biologists are also interested in this debate, and they have not been able to find a genetic basis for intelligence. Jonathan Beckwith, a Harvard microbiologist, says that scientists have not been able to identify the genes (if there are any) that are associated with intelligence (DeParle 1994). Until geneticists are able to find the genes, the idea that intelligence is genetically driven will be suspect. The danger of exploiting and manipulating data for ideological purposes must be taken into account whenever social statistics are given as proof of biological differences.

Given the lack of biological evidence and suspect methodology of those that argue for the predominance of genes, the claims made by those who support the view that environmental factors predominate are, at this time, somewhat stronger. Therefore, there is very little scientific evidence that distributing social goods by merit would lead to the creation of a super-intelligent upper caste that transmits its prized genes to their offspring and shuts out the lower orders from possible upward social mobility. Social mobility is possible for those at the lower end of the social ladder, if they receive sufficient resources and education to make them competitive with the upper classes. This is good news for those that believe that smart, hardworking people, regardless of where they are born, should have a chance to succeed in America. Improving the environments of disadvantaged children would probably have an enormous positive effect in their ability to learn and to score better on intelligence and achievement exams.

Distributive Justice: Incompatible with Market

The next criticism, that meritocracy and markets are incompatible, may be accurate. Interestingly, however, the values that underlie the market as a distributive mechanism are the same values that lay at the core of meritocracy. Most supporters of the free market system justify their positions because the market, in *its* ideal type, is supposed to distribute rewards to intelligent, hardworking individuals. These free market supporters value competition and social mobility. According to Friedman,

> the capital market tend[s] to restrict the more expensive vocational and professional training to individuals whose parents or benefactors can finance the training required. They make such individuals a "non—competing" group sheltered from competition by the unavailability of the necessary capital to many able individuals. The result is to perpetuate inequalities of wealth and status (Friedman 1962, 107).

This outcome conflicts with the values that free market supporters are committed to. However, a program to provide educational resources to the lower classes "would make capital more widely available and would thereby do much to make equality of opportunity a reality, to diminish inequalities of income and wealth, and to promote the full use of our human resources" (Friedman 1962, 107). Supporters of the market system seem to want exactly what a proponent of meritocracy desires: By giving everyone the resources to fully develop their natural capacities, economic efficiency is increased and human capital maximized.

But the free market advocates go on to defend a person's right to transfer their wealth to their children by saying, "it seems illogical to say that a man is entitled to what he has produced by personal capacities or to the produce of the wealth he has accumulated, but that he is not entitled to pass any wealth on to his children; to say that a man may use his income for riotous living but may not give it to his heirs" (Friedman 1962, 164). They then speciously compare receiving an inheritance to serendipitously finding "a $20 bill on the pavement" (Friedman 1962, 165) and make the same unfounded statements about human genetics as Herrnstein and Murray.

One should face severe cognitive dissonance if one values competition, is aware that differences in wealth can create a "'non-competing' group sheltered from competition," and yet support an inheritance system that maintains a sheltered non-competing group. Fortunately, not every proponent of the free market is convinced that inheritances are necessary to maintain a market-based system (Hayek 1944, 113). It is conceivable to have a competitive market-based system without the transmission of wealth along generational lines. Ultimately, more theoretical work will be necessary to reconcile this conflict, if indeed it is possible to be reconciled at all. What can be said is that the values of improving opportunities for the disadvantaged, creating more choices for people, and fostering competition are held in common by both proponents of markets and meritocracy.

Distributive Justice: Too Costly and Harmful

Roemer's views on providing everyone with an equal opportunity to succeed are based on a particularly extreme definition of equal opportunity. Young's meritocracy does not accept this definition; it only attempts to eliminate disadvantages due to race, ethnicity, gender, socio-economic status, and other "irrelevant" characteristics. Once these particular characteristics of birth are compensated for, inequalities in outcome are justified on the basis of differences in natural ability and effort. It certainly would not entail having less able surgeons because in a meritocracy all surgeons would have similar levels of natural ability regardless of their social origins. Meritocracy does not seek to make dumb people smart. It seeks to give smart people without the economic and social resources to succeed the resources to take advantage of their talent and to contribute to society as much as their natural ability allows.

Political Justice

Americans value democracy, but meritocracy, as a political system, need not be undemocratic. Certainly, it would not be a direct democracy where the public votes on laws and policies directly through a ballot because of the public's lack of information and expertise in policy matters, but it could very well be consistent with the system the founders of the American republic envisioned. Ultimately, the idea that meritocracy is undemocratic depends on what one means by democracy.

The founders seemed to have something like a meritocracy in mind. Jefferson believed in the idea of a "natural aristocracy" that could be recruited from all social strata to become America's leaders. It was based on "virtue and talents" and was opposed by the "artificial aristocracy, founded on wealth and birth" (Jefferson 1944, 633). Even patronage, something that is antithetical to meritocracy, had meritocratic ends during the colonial era. At the time, patronage was based on a *noblesse oblige* where men of rank and position would sponsor unusually bright or gifted boys and provide them with the resources to learn the sciences or become involved with politics. Benjamin Franklin, who gained Governor William Keith as a patron, is a wonderful example of this upward mobility. In a system that was closed to many, attempts were made to promote those who were gifted with particular talents.

Some are able to reconcile meritocracy with democratic theory by arguing that democracy is a "by-product of a competitive method of leadership recruitment" (Sartori 1987, 152). We cannot escape the reality that all social systems, even democracies, have concentrated power. What makes democracy distinct from other political systems is that democracy should concentrate power in a selective "polyarchy of merit" (Sartori 1987, 169). Under this view of democracy, there are elections where the meritorious are selected to rule over society. The people remain sovereign but rule indirectly through those they elect.

Dahl's critique stems from the conflation of guardianship and meritocracy. It is true that the meritocratic ideal has its roots in Plato's *Republic*, where a class of guardians would be drawn from all social classes to become the society's leaders. But we need to keep in mind what the ideal imagined. A meritocracy resembles aristocracy in the classical sense of the term meaning "rule by the best." What has happened over the centuries, however, is that aristocracy has become associated with hereditary privilege and a rigid class system. Instead of this, a meritocracy promotes worthy individuals regardless of which social strata they happen to be born in. It does not alienate power from the masses because some individuals from the masses become powerful elites. The system remains open to all classes.

Even if one disagrees with the "polyarchy of merit" concept, one should remember to keep the distinction between meritocracy as a socio-economic idea and meritocracy as a political system in mind. Currently, political scientists sometimes criticize the entire idea when their actual concern is only with a particular conception of the idea. That is, they might criticize meritocracy as a political system without recognizing that meritocracy, as a system of distributive justice, might still be desired and is not harmed by arguments made against the political concept of meritocracy. In the end, those who support meritocracy need not reject democracy as an ideal.

Conclusions

Americans may not be aware of their own value conflicts when issues of merit are raised. Despite the emergence of a "rational public" literature, many scholars still find that that the public is ill-informed and inconsistent in their attitudes, beliefs, and values. When Americans express contradictory views, it is not because they have a theoretically sophisticated framework that rationally distinguishes the two competing views. Usually it is because Americans are not cognizant of the internal contradiction. They've simply never thought about the issue long enough, or in a sufficiently detailed manner, to become aware of the conflict. Nevertheless, we should not hold the American public in too low esteem. With accurate and widely disseminated information, Americans may be able to come to terms with their dissonant views. Public opinion may not be able to tell us what the public "really wants," but the methods employed in this project can give us a glimpse at the conflicts that Americans face when confronted with questions related to meritocracy.

A review of the theoretical literature shows us that there are many values that come into direct conflict when one thinks about meritocracy. Working for what one has may conflict with rewarding intelligent people because natural intelligence is not earned. Giving everyone an equal opportunity may conflict with the notion that parents should favor their own children over the children of others. Favoring the intelligent and hardworking will create an unequal society and, if one supports genetic superiority arguments, lead to a caste system without social mobility. Allowing wealthy individuals the freedom to spoil their offspring conflicts with the ideal that every child should start life with the same chance to succeed. And support for democracy may mean that we should not elevate the smart and hardworking above the common person.

Note

1. Lippmann 1993, 145

Chapter 3

Popular Ideas Concerning Meritocracy

The American dream that we were all raised on is a simple but powerful one—if you work hard and play by the rules you should be given a chance to go as far as your God-given ability will take you.[1]

Bill Clinton

The American dream that President Clinton has in mind is precisely the ideal of meritocracy. It implies that the only limit to one's success in life is their natural capacities. One's race, sex, national origin, and social background should have no impact on a person's outcome in life. Social theorists have critiqued that idea on various grounds, but it remains an ideal that is a permanent fixture of the American creed. Yet, Americans are sometimes skeptical about the ideal and hold beliefs that are in direct conflict with meritocratic values.

The evidence presented in this chapter suggests that Americans are not pure meritocrats; indeed, they are often ambivalent on questions of merit. Hard work is an essential value and there is a strong belief that hard work *should be* rewarded and that it is necessary in order to be successful. In fact, Americans believe that intelligence and hard work *are actually* rewarded. On a variety of measures, Americans hold firm to the meritocratic ethos. But they are also willing to use selection criteria other than merit for the distribution of particular social goods. Indeed, the public believes that one's race, social background, and connections matter for success. In an ideal type meritocracy this would not be the case, and it suggest that Americans are skeptical about the reality of meritocracy.

Support for the Meritocratic Ideal

Lipset argues that Americans strongly subscribe to the meritocratic ethos. "The American Creed" says Lipset, "subsumes classical liberalism, which strongly distrusts the state and emphasizes competitive meritocracy" (Lipset 1996, 144). Citing a NORC survey, he notes that 88% of Americans believe that ambition and hard work are the keys to success. This is opposed to 20% who believed that coming from a wealthy family was critical. Citing a Gallup poll which asks people to choose whether they prefer that historically discriminated-against groups be given preferential treatment to make up for past injustices or choosing

Table 3.1. Hard Work is an Essential Value

(I'm going to read you a list of American ideals. For each please tell me if it is absolutely essential to you personally, important but not essential, or not that important. If you haven't really thought about it much, please say so.) How about the ideal that with hard work, people have a chance to move up and prosper?[1]

Absolutely essential	79%
Important but not essential	20%
Not that important	1%
Haven't thought about it much	1%

(How important is each of the following values to you personally, would you say it is very important, somewhat important, not that important, or not important at all?). . . . Hard work[2]

Very important	83%
Somewhat important	15%
Not that important	1%
Not important at all	1%

(The public schools provide one of the most important ways for teaching our children about the American story. If you were to decide which themes the schools should include, how important would each of the following be in your lesson about America—would it be absolutely essential, very important, somewhat important, somewhat unimportant, very unimportant, or would you definitely leave it out?). . . . With hard work and perseverance, anyone can succeed in America.[3]

Absolutely essential	36%
Very important	47%
Somewhat important	14%
Somewhat unimportant	2%
Very unimportant	1%
Leave it out (vol.)	1%

Sources:
1 *Survey by Public Agenda Foundation, September 3–September 16, 1998.* Retrieved February 22, 2005 from the iPOLL Databank, The Roper Center for Public Opinion Research, University of Connecticut.
2 *Survey by NBC News, Wall Street Journal, Conducted by Hart and Teeter Research Companies, February 26–March 1, 1998.* Retrieved February 22, 2005 from the iPOLL Databank, The Roper Center for Public Opinion Research, University of Connecticut.
3 *Survey by Post-Modernity Project at the University of Virginia, Conducted by Center for Survey Research, University of Virginia, January 27–April 14, 1996.* Retrieved February 22, 2005 from the iPOLL Databank, The Roper Center for Public Opinion Research, University of Connecticut.

Table 3.2. Support for Merit in Pay

How much influence should each of the following have in determining an employee's level of pay?

Employee's level of education[1]

A great deal	33%
Some	55%
Not much	9%
None	4%

Employee's individual effort[2]

A great deal	77%
Some	19%
Not much	2%
None	<1%

Responsibility held by the employee on the job[3]

A great deal	75%
Some	24%
Not much	1%
None	<1%

Being a man and not a woman[4]

A great deal	6%
Some	10%
Not much	14%
None	71%

Sources:
1–3 *Data from the International Social Justice Project (ISJP), International Social Justice Project 1991 [Computer file]. Ann Arbor, MI: Duane F. Alwin, David M. Klingel, and Merilynn Dielman, University of Michigan, Institute for Social Research, Program in Socio-Environmental Studies [producers], 1993.* Ann Arbor, MI: Inter-university Consortium for Political and Social Research. Calculations based on the author's own analysis. Margin of Error +/- 2%
4 *Data from the International Social Justice Project (ISJP), International Social Justice Project 1991 [Computer file]. Ann Arbor, MI: Duane F. Alwin, David M. Klingel, and Merilynn Dielman, University of Michigan, Institute for Social Research, Program in Socio-Environmental Studies [producers], 1993.* Ann Arbor, MI: Inter-university Consortium for Political and Social Research. Calculations based on the author's own analysis. Margin of Error +/- 3%

Table 3.3. Hard Work Leads to Success

(Now let me read you some short statements. Please tell me which statement comes closer to your own view.). . . . Most people who want to get ahead can make it if they're willing to work hard. Hard work and determination are no guarantee of success for most people. (If First/Second statement, ask:) Is that statement much or somewhat closer to your view?[1]

1st Statement Much closer	52%
1st Statement Somewhat closer	20%
2nd Statement Somewhat closer	11%
2nd Statement closer	14%
Both (vol.)	2%
Neither (vol.)	1%
Don't know/Refused	1%

Continued on the next page

Source:
1 *Survey by Children's Research & Education Institute, Conducted by Greenberg Quinlan Rosner Research & Public Opinion Strategies, January 8–January 13, 2003.* Retrieved February 22, 2005 from the iPOLL Databank, The Roper Center for Public Opinion Research, University of Connecticut.

people simply in the basis of their ability for jobs and college entrance, between 81% and 84% believed that ability should be the determining factor (Lipset 1996, 125).

This hard work element of meritocracy should not be underestimated. Tables 3.1 and 3.2 show that the vast majority of Americans believe hard work to be an essential value. It is an idea that is intertwined with their vision of the American dream. It is so important that most Americans want their children to learn that hard work will lead to success while in school. An overwhelming percentage believe that hard work is essential or very important for getting ahead, suggesting that most Americans believe that without hard work a person will almost certainly fail. Most believe that education, hard work, and responsibility should be rewarded with higher pay and that items like gender shouldn't matter. We can begin to see that the popular analog to Young's "Merit = IQ + Effort" is "Merit = Skills and Hard Work."

Consistent with the meritocratic ethos, Americans are fascinated by stories of disadvantaged youths who eventually achieve success. A recent *New York Times* article about the chancellor of New York's public schools, Mr. Klein, describes him as the embodiment of "the postwar meritocracy. His own trajectory—from boyhood in a Queens housing project as the son of a postal worker with a 10th-grade education to degrees from Columbia University and Harvard Law School—relied not on inherited wealth, not on family connections, not on a

Table 3.3. Continued

(I"m going to read you some pairs of statements that will help us understand how you feel about a number of things. As I read each pair, tell me whether the first statement or the second statement comes closer to your own views, even if neither is exactly right.). . . . Most people who want to get ahead can make it if they're willing to work hard. Hard work and determination are no guarantee of success for most people. (After choice is made, ask) Do you feel strongly about that, or not?[2]

Strongly—People can get ahead if they work hard	66%
Not strongly—People can get ahead if they work hard	7%
Strongly—Hard work and determination are no guarantee of success	20%
Not strongly—Hard work and determination are no guarantee of success	4%
Neither/Don't know	1%

(I am going to read several reasons why some people get ahead and succeed in life and others do not. Using a one-to-five scale, where '1' means not at all important and '5' means extremely important, please tell me how important it is as a reason for a person's success. You can choose any number from one to five.) How about hard work and initiative?[3]

1—not at all important	1%
2	1%
3	6%
4	17%
5—extremely important	75%
Don't know	<1%

Sources:
2 *Survey by Pew Research Center, Conducted by Princeton Survey Research Associates, August 24–September 10, 2000.* Retrieved February 22, 2005 from the iPOLL Databank, The Roper Center for Public Opinion Research, University of Connecticut.
3 *Survey by General Motors Corporation, Conducted by Gallup Organization, April 23–May 31, 1998.* Retrieved February 22, 2005 from the iPOLL Databank, The Roper Center for Public Opinion Research, University of Connecticut.

WASP pedigree, but on academic prowess" (Freedman 2004). While such success is becoming more rare, news stories still proliferate and stir the imaginations of ordinary Americans.

These Horatio Alger type stories are a part of American folklore. So much so that Americans tend to believe that they actually live in a meritocracy (Lipset1996, 81). Most Americans adamantly believe that hard work leads to success. Approximately 70% believe that hard work and effort is very important for

Table 3.4. America is a Meritocracy

Are you more or less where you should be in your job, given your talents and effort, or has your hard work been overlooked?[1]

More/less where should be	71%
Hard work/talent overlooked	27%
Don't know/refused	2%

Which is more important in getting ahead—who you know, or what you know?[2]

Who you know	39%
What you know	51%
Equal importance (vol.)	9%
Don't know/Refused	1%

Here are some factors that are sometimes considered important for having high social standing. Please tell me how important each is for success in our society today.

Ability and talent[3]

Very important	49%
Somewhat important	45%
Not very important	5%
Not at all important	1%
Don't know	<1%

Continued on the next page

Sources:

1 *Survey by Reader's Digest, Conducted by Institute for Social Inquiry/Roper Center, University of Connecticut, August 22–August 29, 1994.* Retrieved February 22, 2005 from the iPOLL Databank, The Roper Center for Public Opinion Research, University of Connecticut. Sample consisted of those employed full/part-time.

2 *Survey by Wired, Merrill Lynch, Conducted by Luntz Research Companies during September, 1997.* Retrieved February 22, 2005 from the iPOLL Databank, The Roper Center for Public Opinion Research, University of Connecticut.

3 *Data from the International Social Justice Project (ISJP), International Social Justice Project 1991 [Computer file]. Ann Arbor, MI: Duane F. Alwin, David M. Klingel, and Merilynn Dielman, University of Michigan, Institute for Social Research, Program in Socio-Environmental Studies [producers], 1993.* Ann Arbor, MI: Inter-university Consortium for Political and Social Research. Calculations based on the author's own analysis. Margin of Error +/- 3%

Table 3.4. Continued

Hard work and effort[4]

Very important	70%
Somewhat important	27%
Not very important	4%
Not at all important	<1%

Source:
4 *Data from the International Social Justice Project (ISJP), International Social Justice Project 1991 [Computer file]. Ann Arbor, MI: Duane F. Alwin, David M. Klingel, and Merilynn Dielman, University of Michigan, Institute for Social Research, Program in Socio-Environmental Studies [producers], 1993.* Ann Arbor, MI: Inter-university Consortium for Political and Social Research. Calculations based on the author's own analysis. Margin of Error +/- 3%

Table 3.5. Effort, Ability, and Economic Success

How often is each of the following factors a reason for why there are rich people in this country today? Hard work?[1]

Very often	26%
Often	41%
Sometimes	24%
Rarely	8%
Never	1%

How often is each of the following factors a reason for why there are rich people in this country today? Ability or talent[2]

Very often	21%
Often	40%
Sometimes	32%
Rarely	7%
Never	1%

Sources:
1–2 *Data from the International Social Justice Project (ISJP), International Social Justice Project 1991 [Computer file]. Ann Arbor, MI: Duane F. Alwin, David M. Klingel, and Merilynn Dielman, University of Michigan, Institute for Social Research, Program in Socio-Environmental Studies [producers], 1993.* Ann Arbor, MI: Inter-university Consortium for Political and Social Research. Calculations based on the author's own analysis. Margin of Error +/- 3%

Table 3.6. Social Status is Attained through Hard Work

I'm going to read a list of some of the top positions in our society. For each one, would you tell me the reason you think most people reach them—is it because of chance, say the type of family you're born into, who you know, etc., or is it more due to talent, hard work and a strong will on the part of the individuals to reach those positions in spite of chance? Do you think more people get to be ________ because of who they are and who they know, or more get there because of hard work, talent and strong will?

Successful professional people such as doctors, lawyers, architects, etc.[1]

Who are, who know	9%
Hard work	87%

Successful people in the arts[2]

Who are, who know	15%
Hard work	76%

Major T.V., radio and newspaper commentators[3]

Who are, who know	26%
Hard work	66%

When an athlete is successful, is it mostly because of natural ability or mostly because of hard work?[4]

Natural ability	19%
Hard work	49%
Both equally	31%

Sources:
1–3 *Survey conducted by Roper Organization, January 11–January 25, 1986.* Retrieved March 15, 2005 from the iPOLL Databank, The Roper Center for Public Opinion Research, University of Connecticut.
4 *Survey by USA Today, NBC News, conducted by Gordon S. Black Corporation, July 29–August 14, 1990.* Retrieved March 15, 2005 from the iPOLL Databank, The Roper Center for Public Opinion Research, University of Connecticut

achieving high social standing in America and most Americans believe that "what you know" is more important than "who you know" for getting ahead. Sixty-seven percent of Americans believe that hard work is often or very often the reason for why people are rich in America. Over 60% of Americans believe that ability or talent is the reason people are rich. There is a great deal of data that supports Lipset's claims about the meritocratic ethos in America.

The vast majority of Americans believe that successful doctors, lawyers, architects, artists, television and radio commentators, and athletes reach these top positions in society because of their hard work, talent, and strong will; not

Table 3.7. Social Inequality is Fair

Here are different opinions about social differences in this country. Please tell me for each one whether you strongly agree, somewhat agree, somewhat disagree, or strongly disagree.

Differences in social standing between people are acceptable because they basically reflect what people made out of the opportunities they had.[1]

Strongly agree	17%
Somewhat agree	57%
Somewhat disagree	21%
Strongly disagree	5%

All in all, I think social differences in this country are justified.[2]

Strongly agree	9%
Somewhat agree	45%
Somewhat disagree	34%
Strongly disagree	12%

It is just that people in some occupations are regarded more highly than people in other ones.[3]

Strongly agree	26%
Somewhat agree	43%
Neither agree or disagree	6%
Somewhat disagree	14%
Strongly disagree	11%

Sources:
1 *Data from National Opinion Research Center (NORC), The University of Chicago, General Social Survey (GSS) 1984, Cumulative GSS data file 1972–2002 [Computer file].* Ann Arbor, MI: Inter-university Consortium for Political and Social Research. Calculations based on the author's own analysis. Margin of Error +/- 2%
2 *Data from National Opinion Research Center (NORC), The University of Chicago, General Social Survey (GSS) 1984, Cumulative GSS data file 1972–2002 [Computer file].* Ann Arbor, MI: Inter-university Consortium for Political and Social Research. Calculations based on the author's own analysis. Margin of Error +/- 3%
3 *Data from the International Social Justice Project (ISJP), International Social Justice Project 1991 [Computer file]. Ann Arbor, MI: Duane F. Alwin, David M. Klingel, and Merilynn Dielman, University of Michigan, Institute for Social Research, Program in Socio-Environmental Studies [producers], 1993.* Ann Arbor, MI: Inter-university Consortium for Political and Social Research. Calculations based on the author's own analysis. Margin of Error +/- 4%

Table 3.8. Political Power: What Matters and What Doesn't

If a candidate for public official is a woman, does that make you more, or less likely to vote for that candidate?[1]

More likely	18%
Less likely	10%
No effect	68%
Don't know	3%

On the whole, men make better political leaders than women do.[2]

Strongly agree	7%
Agree	27%
Disagree	51%
Strongly disagree	15%

Do you feel that people are best represented in politics by leaders from their own racial or ethnic background, or doesn't the leader's background make very much difference?[3]

Leaders from own background	35%
Leaders background doesn't matter	65%

Continued on the next page

Sources:
1 *Survey conducted by Penn & Schoen Associates, August 26–August 30, 1983.* Retrieved March 15, 2005 from the iPOLL Databank, The Roper Center for Public Opinion Research, University of Connecticut.
2 *Data from the World Values Survey (WVS) 1995, WVS 1981–1984, 1990–1993, and 1995–1997 [Computer file], ICPSR version. Ann Arbor, MI: Ronald Inglehart, et. al., Institute for Social Research [producer], 1999.* Ann Arbor, MI: Inter-university Consortium for Political and Social Research [distributor], 2003. Calculations based on the author's own analysis. Margin of Error +/- 3%
3 *Data from National Opinion Research Center (NORC), The University of Chicago, General Social Survey (GSS) 1991, Cumulative GSS data file 1972–2002 [Computer file].* Ann Arbor, MI: Inter-university Consortium for Political and Social Research. Calculations based on the author's own analysis. Margin of Error +/- 2%

because of chance, the type of family they are born into, or who they know. But even if some people are harder working or more talented than others, is it really fair to hold some people in higher regard than others? Wouldn't we prefer to all be equals? The fact is that there is a tendency for many Americans to agree that it is fair for some people to be regarded more highly than others. They believe

Table 3.8. Continued

Some people say that it is only fair that in a society like ours, people holding public office should have roughly the same racial or ethnic background as the population as a whole. So, for example, if 30% of the people were Hispanic, then 30% of the public officials should be Hispanic as well. Others say that in choosing people for public office they should be considered purely on the basis of ability without regard to their ethnic or racial background. Let me ask you about these ideas in several different areas. What about people in Congress? Should they have the same racial or ethnic background as their constituents, or should they be considered purely on the basis of their ability without regard to their racial or ethnic background?[4]

Consider ethnic background	9%
Ability, not background	91%

Source:
4 *Data from National Opinion Research Center (NORC), The University of Chicago, General Social Survey (GSS) 1991, Cumulative GSS data file 1972–2002 [Computer file].* Ann Arbor, MI: Inter-university Consortium for Political and Social Research. Calculations based on the author's own analysis. Margin of Error +/- 1%

that differences in social status are justified and that differences in social status are a reflection of what people did with the opportunities they had.

Americans also seem to draw on meritocratic norms when they select their public officials. Most Americans say that the fact that a candidate is a woman has no effect on their vote choice. They also do not believe that men make better political leaders than women. When deciding who would best represent the interests of minorities, Americans reject the idea that only members of the same racial or ethnic group as their constituents can satisfy that need. A majority believes that a political leader's ethnic or racial background doesn't matter. They also reject of the idea of racially proportional representation in the Congress. Americans believe that US representatives should be chosen purely on the basis of their ability regardless of the ethnic or racial composition of their constituents. This is entirely in line with the idea that merit, instead gender or race, should be the decisive factor in choosing our elected officials.

If intelligence and academic prowess, aside from hard work, are also supposed to lead to success, then Americans' views on intelligence should be discussed in light of the concerns brought up in chapter 2. The public, unlike many of those in academia, are not very concerned about the role of genetics in society. Table 3.9 suggests that an overwhelming majority of Americans believe that racial differences are cultural rather than genetic. It also shows that the public leans slightly toward environmental reasons when asked if genes or the environ-

Table 3.9. Success, Genes, and Intelligence

I am going to read you a list of some concerns that some people have expressed about aspects of life in America. Please tell me which of these is of greatest concern to you . . . the weakening of traditional family values, high taxes, high government spending, finding good jobs and economic opportunity, the need for better and safer schools, addressing the problem of income inequality, the need for a cleaner environment, America's competitiveness in the world economy, preserving Medicare and Social Security for the future, emerging new issues around the role of science, technology, and genetics, or crime and violence?[1]

Weakening traditional family values	20%
Preserving Medicare and Social Security	15%
Need for better and safer schools	15%
Crime and violence	14%
Finding good jobs and economic opportunity	7%
High government spending	6%
High taxes	5%
Need for cleaner environment	5%
New issues around the role of science, technology and genetics	4%
Addressing problem of income inequality	3%
America's competitiveness in world economy	3%
Don't know	3%

Overall, do you think that racial and ethnic differences are mostly due to culture and family upbringing or mostly due to heredity and genes?[2]

Culture/Upbringing	88%
Heredity/Genes	6%
Both (vol.)	3%
Neither (vol.)	1%
Don't know/Refused	2%

Continued on the next page

Sources:
1 *Survey by Democratic Leadership Council, Conducted by Penn, Schoen & Berland Associates, July 30–August 2, 1998.* Retrieved March 15, 2005 from the iPOLL Databank, The Roper Center for Public Opinion Research, University of Connecticut.
2 *Survey by U.S.News & World Report, Bozell Worldwide, Conducted by KRC Communications/Research, February 6–February 9, 1997.* Retrieved March 15, 2005 from the iPOLL Databank, The Roper Center for Public Opinion Research, University of Connecticut.

ment have a larger role in determining a person's intelligence. When your average American says that smart, hardworking people should be successful, he does not imagine that such an idea will lead to a genetically determined caste system.

Table 3.9. Continued

(Character, personality, success or failure, and many other types of behaviors are thought to be influenced by both the genes you inherited from your parents and what you learn and experience as you grow up. For each of the following, please say whether you think it is more dependent on the genes you inherit or more from what you learn and experience.). . . . Intelligence[3]

Genes you inherit	45%
Learning and experience	52%
Not sure	4%

(Character, personality, success or failure, and many other types of behaviors are thought to be influenced by both the genes you inherited from your parents and what you learn and experience as you grow up. For each of the following, please say whether you think it is more dependent on the genes you inherit or more from what you learn and experience.). . . . Success in life[4]

Genes you inherit	8%
Learning and experience	90%
Not sure	3%

It is just luck if some people are more intelligent or skillful than others, so they don't deserve to earn more money.[5]

Strongly agree	3%
Somewhat agree	11%
Neither agree or disagree	6%
Somewhat disagree	29%
Strongly disagree	52%
Don't know	1%

Sources:
3 *Survey by Louis Harris & Associates, July 13–July 16, 1995.* Retrieved March 15, 2005 from the iPOLL Databank, The Roper Center for Public Opinion Research, University of Connecticut.
4 *Survey by Louis Harris & Associates, July 13–July 16, 1995.* Retrieved March 15, 2005 from the iPOLL Databank, The Roper Center for Public Opinion Research, University of Connecticut.
5 *Data from the International Social Justice Project (ISJP), International Social Justice Project 1991 [Computer file]. Ann Arbor, MI: Duane F. Alwin, David M. Klingel, and Merilynn Dielman, University of Michigan, Institute for Social Research, Program in Socio-Environmental Studies [producers], 1993.* Ann Arbor, MI: Inter-university Consortium for Political and Social Research. Calculations based on the author's own analysis. Margin of Error +/- 3%

Table 3.10. Skepticism in Meritocracy

(I am going to read you a series of statements that describe America today. For each one, please tell me, how much truth there is for each one—a great deal of truth, a fair amount of truth, not very much truth or no truth at all in the statement.). . . . Our nation is facing a decline in people taking personal responsibility, with too many people relying on government handouts and programs rather than working and being self-sufficient. The money spent on lawsuits has increased to over two hundred billion dollars a year, as people try to blame others and win a windfall in court. We've lost the link between taking responsibility, hard work and success. [1]

A great deal of truth	53%
A fair amount of truth	30%
Not very much truth	14%
No truth at all	2%

(Here are some statements that people have made about why some individuals aren't working as hard as they could. For each one, please tell me whether you strongly agree, slightly agree, slightly disagree, or strongly disagree.). . . . People simply don't believe that hard work pays off anymore[2]

Strongly agree	28%
Slightly agree	35%
Slightly disagree	22%
Strongly disagree	14%
Not sure/Don't know	1%

[In the US] people get what they need.[3]

Strongly agree	5%
Somewhat agree	35%
Neither agree or disagree	9%
Somewhat disagree	33%
Strongly disagree	17%
Don't know	1%

Sources:
1 *Survey by Public Interest Project. Methodology: Conducted by Greenberg Quinlan Rosner Research, April 5–April 8, 2004.* Retrieved February 22, 2005 from the iPOLL Databank, The Roper Center for Public Opinion Research, University of Connecticut.
2 *Survey by Public Agenda Foundation during June, 1982 and based on personal interviews with a people employed more than 20 hours/week.* Retrieved February 22, 2005 from the iPOLL Databank, The Roper Center for Public Opinion Research, University of Connecticut.
3 *Data from the International Social Justice Project (ISJP), International Social Justice Project 1991 [Computer file]. Ann Arbor, MI: Duane F. Alwin, David M. Klingel, and Merilynn Dielman, University of Michigan, Institute for Social Research, Program in Socio-Environmental Studies [producers], 1993.* Ann Arbor, MI: Inter-university Consortium for Political and Social Research. Calculations based on the author's own analysis.

Table 3.11. Connections and Opportunities in Economic Success

How often is each of the following factors a reason for why there are rich people in this country today?

Having the right connections[1]

Very often	32%
Often	43%
Sometimes	22%
Rarely	3%
Never	<1%

More opportunities to begin with[2]

Very often	24%
Often	39%
Sometimes	29%
Rarely	8%
Never	<1%

Source:
1–2 *Data from the International Social Justice Project (ISJP), International Social Justice Project 1991 [Computer file]. Ann Arbor, MI: Duane F. Alwin, David M. Klingel, and Merilynn Dielman, University of Michigan, Institute for Social Research, Program in Socio-Environmental Studies [producers], 1993.* Ann Arbor, MI: Inter-university Consortium for Political and Social Research. Calculations based on the author's own analysis. Margin of Error +/- 3%

Success is not connected to a person's genes in the minds of most Americans. Most importantly, Americans flatly reject the Rawlsian argument that intelligent people don't deserve more money because being intelligent is a result of good luck. A majority of Americans support the idea that more intelligent people deserve more money. These findings suggest that most Americans are more supportive of meritocracy than the intellectual critics of it.

Rejecting Meritocracy

The information available from various surveys also suggests that there is some skepticism about the reality of meritocracy among the American populace. The evidence on Table 3.10 suggests that most Americans believe that "we've lost the link" between hard work and success, particularly after being given informa-

Table 3.12. Why are Economic Leaders Successful?

I'm going to read a list of some of the top positions in our society. For each one, would you tell me the reason you think most people reach them—is it because of chance, say the type of family you're born into, who you know, etc., or is it more due to talent, hard work and a strong will on the part of the individuals to reach those positions in spite of chance?

Do you think more people get to be heads of the country's big labor unions because of who they are and who they know, or more get there because of hard work, talent and strong will?[1]

Who are, who know	54%
Hard work	36%
Don't know	10%

Do you think more people get to be millionaires because of who they are and who they know, or more get there because of hard work, talent and strong will?[2]

Who are, who know	49%
Hard work	40%
Don't know	10%

Sources:
1–2 *Survey conducted by Roper Organization, January 11–January 25, 1986.* Retrieved March 15, 2005 from the iPOLL Databank, The Roper Center for Public Opinion Research, University of Connecticut.

tion about people winning large lawsuit settlements. Americans probably view the acquisition of wealth from lawsuits as "non-work" and therefore contrary to the meritocratic ideal. A majority of Americans are even willing to acknowledge that not everyone may believe that hard work leads to success. In addition, many Americans are not convinced that everyone gets what they need. This may lead us to conclude that perhaps we should be skeptical about equal opportunity; after all, if a person doesn't have what they need, they certainly aren't on a level playing field with those who do.

In a meritocracy one's personal connections should not matter. 75% of Americans, however, believe that having the right connections is a reason for why people are rich in America. This suggests that most Americans understand that technical merit alone is not the sole reason why people are successful. 63% of Americans believe that having more opportunities to begin with is often or very often a reason why people are rich. This too suggests that Americans understand that effort and ability are not the only factors that contribute to economic success.

Table 3.13. Social Status Not Based on Merit

Here are some factors that are sometimes considered important for having high social standing. Please tell me how important each is for success in our society today.

Social background[1]

Very important	24%
Somewhat important	51%
Not very important	19%
Not at all important	6%

Having the right connections[2]

Very important	39%
Somewhat important	45%
Not very important	11%
Not at all important	5%

One's sex[3]

Very important	10%
Somewhat important	38%
Not very important	32%
Not at all important	21%

Belonging to a particular ethnic or racial group[4]

Very important	14%
Somewhat important	35%
Not very important	29%
Not at all important	22%

Sources:
1–4 *Data from the International Social Justice Project (ISJP), International Social Justice Project 1991 [Computer file]. Ann Arbor, MI: Duane F. Alwin, David M. Klingel, and Merilynn Dielman, University of Michigan, Institute for Social Research, Program in Socio-Environmental Studies [producers], 1993.* Ann Arbor, MI: Inter-university Consortium for Political and Social Research. Calculations based on the author's own analysis. Margin of Error +/- 3%

When it comes to high-level economic actors, Americans are not convinced that those individuals have attained their positions strictly through hard work;

Table 3.14. What Leads to Political Success?

Now I want to read you some things that have been said about politics and politicians. Tell me, for each, whether you tend to agree or disagree. Most jobs in politics are not given on merit.[1]

Agree	63%
Disagree	17%
Not sure	20%

I'm going to read a list of some of the top positions in our society. For each one, would you tell me the reason you think most people reach them—is it because of chance, say the type of family you're born into, who you know, etc., or is it more due to talent, hard work and a strong will on the part of the individuals to reach those positions in spite of chance? Do you think more people get to be important political leaders such as President, state Governor, or U.S. Senator because of who they are and who they know, or more get there because of hard work, talent and strong will?[2]

Who are, who know	60%
Hard work	35%
Don't know	6%

Continued on the next page

Sources:
1 *Survey conducted by Louis Harris & Associates during September 1971.* Retrieved March 15, 2005 from the iPOLL Databank, The Roper Center for Public Opinion Research, University of Connecticut.
2 *Survey conducted by Roper Organization, January 11–January 25, 1986.* Retrieved March 15, 2005 from the iPOLL Databank, The Roper Center for Public Opinion Research, University of Connecticut.

family background and social capital are believed to play important roles. A majority of Americans believe that the heads of the country's big labor unions have attained their position because of the type of family they're born into and who they know and not because of their talent, hard work, or strong will. A plurality believes the same is true of millionaires. It seems that Americans are faced with contradictory beliefs about what causes one to be successful in America today.

If America was truly a meritocracy, then one's social background would have no effect on one's achieved status. In this regard as well Americans reject the notion of meritocracy. A majority believes that social background is impor-

Table 3.14. Continued

In general, do you think most members of Congress work hard, or not?[3]

Work hard	48%
Don't work hard	47%
Don't know/No answer	5%

Which one or two of the following aspects, if any, would concern you the most about working for the federal government? Decisions being based on politics instead of merit, too much bureaucracy, poor performers not being dismissed, low pay, few opportunities for advancement, not being appreciated or respected by the public, or work that is not interesting.[4]
Note: Adds to more than 100% due to multiple responses

Decisions being based on politics instead of merit	47%
Too much bureaucracy	37%
Poor performers not being dismissed	24%
Low pay	13%
New opportunities for advancement	9%
Not being appreciated or respected by the public	9%
Work that is not interesting	7%
None/other	1%
Not sure	3%

Continued on the next page

Sources:
3 *Survey conducted by CBS News/New York Times, October 29–November 1, 1994.* Retrieved March 15, 2005 from the iPOLL Databank, The Roper Center for Public Opinion Research, University of Connecticut.
4 *Survey by Council for Excellence in Government, Partnership for Public Service, conducted by Hart and Teeter Research Companies, July 31–August 8, 2001.* Retrieved March 15, 2005 from the iPOLL Databank, The Roper Center for Public Opinion Research, University of Connecticut.

tant for having a high social status. An extraordinary 84% believe that having the right connections is critical for attaining high social status. Race and sex, which should have no effect on social status in a meritocracy, are not rejected as factors in the attainment of high social status. It appears that non-merit factors are believed to be influencing one's place in the social hierarchy. This stands in opposition to notions of a fully meritocratic social structure in the US and directly contradicts the Horatio Alger ideal that one's social origins are irrelevant in achieving success.

Table 3.14. Continued

During the (1976 Presidential) campaign, President Carter promised to appoint United States Attorneys and judges strictly on the basis of merit, without regard for political considerations. Do you think he has kept his promise on this or not?[5]

Yes	20%
No	52%
Not sure	28%

Now let me read you some statements that some people have made about Senator Edward Kennedy. For each statement, tell me if you agree or disagree. He has gotten as far as he has because of his name.[6]

Agree	51%
Disagree	43%
Not sure	6%

Sources:
5 *Survey conducted by NBC News, February 21–February 22, 1978.* Retrieved March 15, 2005 from the iPOLL Databank, The Roper Center for Public Opinion Research, University of Connecticut.
6 *Survey conducted by ABC News/Louis Harris and Associates, December 21–December 26, 1978.* Retrieved March 15, 2005 from the iPOLL Databank, The Roper Center for Public Opinion Research, University of Connecticut.

We may also be interested in testing Dahl's criticism that meritocracy is undemocratic. Even though Americans want their public officials to be selected on the basis of merit, Americans do not believe this is how decisions are actually made. Americans believe that most jobs in politics are decided by political considerations instead of merit. They believe that important political leaders attain their position because of who they know instead of through hard work. Indeed, Americans are not convinced that their Congressional representatives work hard. When the public is asked what is the most important problem facing the bureaucracy, a plurality believes that too many decisions are based on politics instead of merit. This has been true for some time; Americans believe that Carter's judicial appointments were made because of political considerations instead of on the basis of merit and that Edward Kennedy has attained his position because of his name.

The Jeffersonian ideal of a "natural aristocracy" taking the reigns of the American republic isn't supported by a majority of Americans today. Knowing that there are many decisions in which it is impossible to please everyone, Americans would like public officials to consult experts in order to do what is best for the country. However, a majority of Americans believe it is a bad idea if

Table 3.15. Role of Experts in Government

Public officials often have to make decisions in which it is impossible to please everyone. Under these circumstances, which do you think they ought to do: try to work out a compromise that gives everyone at least something or do what experts think is best for the country as a whole, even though some people may be satisfied and others hurt by the decision?[1]

Work out a compromise that gives everyone something	37%
Do what experts think is best for country	54%
About equally important	2%
Neither	3%
Don't know	4%

I'm going to describe various types of political systems and ask what you think about each as a way of governing this country. For each one, would you say it is a very good, fairly good, fairly bad, or very bad way of governing?

Having experts, not government, make decisions according to what they think is best for the country[2]

Very good	8%
Fairly good	28%
Fairly bad	29%
Very bad	35%

Having a democratic political system[3]

Very good	55%
Fairly good	36%
Fairly bad	6%
Very bad	3%

Sources:
1 *Survey conducted by Market Strategies, May 3–May 5, 1999.* Retrieved March 15, 2005 from the iPOLL Databank, The Roper Center for Public Opinion Research, University of Connecticut.
2 *Data from the World Values Survey (WVS) 1995, WVS 1981–1984, 1990–1993, and 1995–1997 [Computer file], ICPSR version. Ann Arbor, MI: Ronald Inglehart, et. al., Institute for Social Research [producer], 1999.* Ann Arbor, MI: Inter-university Consortium for Political and Social Research [distributor], 2003. Calculations based on the author's own analysis. Margin of Error +/- 3%
3 *Data from the World Values Survey (WVS) 1995, WVS 1981–1984, 1990–1993, and 1995–1997 [Computer file], ICPSR version. Ann Arbor, MI: Ronald Inglehart, et. al., Institute for Social Research [producer], 1999.* Ann Arbor, MI: Inter-university Consortium for Political and Social Research [distributor], 2003. Calculations based on the author's own analysis. Margin of Error +/- 2%

Table 3.16. Support for Non-Merit Factors in Pay

How much influence should each of the following have in determining an employee's level of pay?

Length of service with the employer[1]

A great deal	48%
Some	45%
Not much	4%
None	2%

Unpleasant working conditions such as dirty, noisy, or strenuous work[2]

A great deal	42%
Some	48%
Not much	7%
None	4%

Continued on the next page

Sources:
1–2 *Data from the International Social Justice Project (ISJP), International Social Justice Project 1991 [Computer file]. Ann Arbor, MI: Duane F. Alwin, David M. Klingel, and Merilynn Dielman, University of Michigan, Institute for Social Research, Program in Socio-Environmental Studies [producers], 1993.* Ann Arbor, MI: Inter-university Consortium for Political and Social Research. Calculations based on the author's own analysis. Margin of Error +/- 2%

experts had direct control over the government. At first it may seem a peculiar idea to have non-experts rule the country, but the key to this view is not that experts be un-influential, rather it is the expectation and preference that the government submit to the public's preferences and to do what is best for the nation. In this sense, the public is strongly in favor of democracy and willing to heed Dahl's concern that a political meritocracy is undemocratic.

The vast majority (73%) disagree with the statement that a poor person has the same chance for a fair trial as a wealthy person.[2] This means that most Americans are aware of wealth differences and acknowledge that wealth can skew one's ability to act as a citizen on equal terms with others. Yet, there is also the widely held belief that America provides an equal opportunity for all. If we chose to define equal opportunity as the lack of legal/political barriers, then this shows ambivalence on the part of the public. Americans understand that opportunities for a fair trial depend on one's economic resources, but this seems to have no bearing on their perception of America as the land of (equal) opportunity.

If Americans value meritocracy, then how could we tolerate such an unmeritocratic reality? In part it is because American values reject the meritocratic

Table 3.16. Continued

There has been a lot of discussion lately about whether salary increases, when offered, should be distributed equally to all employees, or whether employees who perform well during the year deserve merit pay increases which are bigger than the increases given to other employees. Which of these statements comes closest to your point of view on this issue?[3]

All employees should receive the same minimum percentage of salary increase, with additional increases to be determined on the basis of merit—that is, employees who have performed well during the past year would get a larger increase than other employees	52%
All salary increases should be determined on the basis of merit—that is only employees who have performed well during the past year would receive a salary increase	33%
All employees should receive the same percentage of salary increase regardless of how well they have performed during the past year	12%

Sources:
3 *Survey conducted by Roper Organization, May 31–June 7, 1986.* Retrieved March 15, 2005 from the iPOLL Databank, The Roper Center for Public Opinion Research, University of Connecticut.

ideal. A very strong (64%) majority of Americans believe it is fair for those who can afford a better education for their children to provide it.[3] This is a remarkably unmeritocratic response. Distributing education through the market, so that the wealthy acquire better schooling, violates the very core of meritocratic justice. They support pay based on seniority and on the pleasantness of the working conditions, which is quite different from pay based on merit. And, when asked if salary increases should be based on merit only, or be distributed equally to all employees, a majority chooses a mixture of the two. Overall, Americans are not fully committed to meritocracy. They are sometimes ready to ignore or reject meritocratic values in favor of other more salient ones.

Racial Divisions

There are many questions that may be answered differently depending on one's group affiliation. Why are some people successful? Because of merit or favoritism? Why do social differences exist? Is it because of differences in effort or because of limited opportunities and economic circumstances? Why are some

Table 3.17. Educational Advantages for the Wealthy

It is just that those who can afford it obtain a better education for their children.[1]

	Whites	African Americans	χ^2	Cramer's V
			53.5**	.098**
Strongly agree	29%	57%		
Somewhat agree	34%	25%		
Neither agree or disagree	6%	<1%		
Somewhat disagree	17%	10%		
Strongly disagree	14%	7%		

*p < .05 ** p < .01
Source:
1 *Data from the International Social Justice Project (ISJP), International Social Justice Project 1991 [Computer file]. Ann Arbor, MI: Duane F. Alwin, David M. Klingel, and Merilynn Dielman, University of Michigan, Institute for Social Research, Program in Socio-Environmental Studies [producers], 1993.* Ann Arbor, MI: Inter-university Consortium for Political and Social Research. Calculations based on the author's own analysis.

people rich and others poor? Is it due to dishonesty and loose morals, ability and talent, hard work, or one's connections? The old adage "Where one stands depends on where one sits" suggests that differences of opinion on these questions will be related to one's social circumstances.

Because the issue of race has been at the center of political debate in the US since this country's founding, we should expect that different racial and ethnic groups have differing opinions regarding merit and opportunity. They may disagree over the idea that the US offers equal opportunities for everyone or the extent to which racism is a problem. One may reasonably expect that blacks and whites have different opinions about these questions because of their different histories and group interests. African Americans, of course, have faced legal barriers that restricted opportunities for advancement, while whites enjoyed special privileges. Individuals from these two groups "sit" in different places in our society.

A good deal of work has already been conducted on the matter of race and distributive justice. Remember that one major tenet of the meritocratic ethos is the belief that everyone who works hard can reasonably anticipate success. From this it might follow that those who are unsuccessful *ipso facto* lack the Protestant work ethic—they are unmeritorious. Upper-class African Americans are especially likely to believe, however, that effort has little to do with their success or failure. Instead, they tend to believe that ascriptive characteristics have had a strong influence on their place in society. This violates the principles of

Table 3.18. Differences Over Opportunity and Discrimination

In the US people have equal opportunities to get ahead.[1]

	Whites	African Americans	χ^2	Cramer's V
			53.7**	.098**
Strongly agree	16%	19%		
Somewhat agree	51%	31%		
Neither agree or disagree	5%	4%		
Somewhat disagree	21%	27%		
Strongly disagree	7%	19%		

Continued on the next page

*p < .05 ** p < .01
Source:
1 *Data from the International Social Justice Project (ISJP), International Social Justice Project 1991 [Computer file]. Ann Arbor, MI: Duane F. Alwin, David M. Klingel, and Merilynn Dielman, University of Michigan, Institute for Social Research, Program in Socio-Environmental Studies [producers], 1993.* Ann Arbor, MI: Inter-university Consortium for Political and Social Research. Calculations based on the author's own analysis.

meritocracy and researchers have found that their belief in the "American Dream" is compromised (Hochschild 1995, 73). Whites, on the other hand, are especially likely to believe that all Americans have an equal opportunity to become successful (Hochschild 1995, 68). Other researchers dealing with issues of distributive justice have found that those with favorable outcomes are more likely to consider the process and the outcome to be fair (Tyler 1986). Advantaged groups, whites in this case, should be more likely to believe that the system, or *status quo*, is just.

In a meritocracy racial discrimination is totally eliminated and people are rewarded for their effort. In many ways whites and African Americans are equally likely to believe that the US is in fact a meritocratic society. Just like the white population, the vast majority of African Americans believe that people are rewarded for their effort. They believe that decisions about who is hired, promoted, or admitted to college should be based strictly on merit rather than race or ethnicity. Huge majorities of both groups agree that it is important to help the less fortunate. Contrary to expectations, however, there are no significant differences by race on the question of whether one's race is important for high social standing. African Americans are just as divided over this question as whites, some believe race matters and others do not. As stated earlier a majority of both blacks and whites believe that those who can afford it should obtain a better

Table 3.18. Continued

Do you feel that African Americans have more, less, or about the same opportunities in life as whites have?[2]

	Whites	African Americans	χ^2	Cramer's V
			212.4**	.176**
More opportunity	13%	1%		
Less opportunity	27%	74%		
About the same	58%	23%		

Now please tell me how much discrimination there is against each of these groups in our society today. How about African Americans? Would you say there is a lot of discrimination, some, only a little, or none at all?[3]

	Whites	African Americans	χ^2	Cramer's V
			133.6**	.125**
A lot of discrimination	20%	48%		
Some	52%	39%		
Only a little	17%	9%		
None at all	8%	2%		

Continued on the next page

*p < .05 ** p < .01
Source:
2–3 *Survey by Washington Post, Henry J. Kaiser Family Foundation, Harvard University, March 29–May 20, 2001.* Retrieved November 16, 2005 from the iPOLL Databank, The Roper Center for Public Opinion Research, University of Connecticut. Calculations based on the author's own analysis.

education for their children. Somewhat surprisingly, however, African Americans are more likely to hold this view than whites.

In other respects African Americans and whites do show significant differences of opinion. Although 68% of whites believe that America provides equal opportunity only 50% of African Americans believe the same. When both groups were asked specifically about African Americans the results were far more disparate. A majority of whites believe that African Americans have about the same opportunities in life as whites, while 74% of African Americans believe they have less opportunity. The two groups disagree about whether the

Table 3.18. Continued

Thinking specifically about African Americans, do you think the average African American is better off, worse off, or just about as well off as the average white person in terms of (READ ITEM)? Is that a lot better/worse off or just a little?

Income[4]

	Whites	African Americans	χ^2	Cramer's V
			221.4**	.147**
A lot better off	2%	3%		
A little better off	3%	7%		
A little worse off	39%	30%		
A lot worse off	18%	42%		
Just about as well off	37%	15%		

Access to health care[5]

	Whites	African Americans	χ^2	Cramer's V
			135.6**	.126**
A lot better off	6%	4%		
A little better off	5%	4%		
A little worse off	23%	25%		
A lot worse off	12%	36%		
Just about as well off	51%	26%		

Continued on the next page

*p < .05 ** p < .01
Source:
4–5 *Survey by Washington Post, Henry J. Kaiser Family Foundation, Harvard University, March 29–May 20, 2001.* Retrieved November 16, 2005 from the iPOLL Databank, The Roper Center for Public Opinion Research, University of Connecticut. Calculations based on the author's own analysis.

federal government should make sure that jobs are of equal quality, with whites believing it isn't the government's role.

Majorities of both whites and African Americans believe that the federal government has the responsibility to make sure that minorities have the same

Table 3.18. Continued

Education[6]

	Whites	African Americans	χ^2 158.2**	Cramer's V .136**
A lot better off	3%	5%		
A little better off	5%	6%		
A little worse off	33%	29%		
A lot worse off	16%	31%		
Just about as well off	42%	26%		

The types of jobs they have[7]

	Whites	African Americans	χ^2 214.1**	Cramer's V .158**
A lot better off	1%	4%		
A little better off	4%	5%		
A little worse off	33%	26%		
A lot worse off	16%	42%		
Just about as well off	44%	23%		

Which of the following comes closer to your opinion?[8]

	Whites	African Americans	χ^2 120.8**	Cramer's V .124**
We have overcome the major problems facing racial minorities in this country	34%	9%		
There are still major problems facing racial minorities in this country	63%	88%		

*p < .05 ** p < .01

Sources:

6–8 *Survey by Washington Post, Henry J. Kaiser Family Foundation, Harvard University, March 29–May 20, 2001.* Retrieved November 16, 2005 from the iPOLL Databank, The Roper Center for Public Opinion Research, University of Connecticut. Calculations based on the author's own analysis.

Table 3.19. Differences in Reasons for Poverty

Now I'm going to read you some pairs of statements that will help us understand how you feel about a number of things. As I read each pair, tell me whether the first statement or the second statement comes closer to your own views—even if neither is exactly right.[1]

Statement #1: Racial discrimination is the main reason why many black people can't get ahead these days
Statement #2: Blacks who can't get ahead in this country are mostly responsible for their own condition

	Whites	African Americans	χ^2	Cramer's V
			166.8**	.119**
#1 strongly	19%	43%		
#1 not strongly	10%	7%		
#2 not strongly	44%	30%		
#2 strongly	13%	5%		
Neither/Both equally	8%	10%		

Continued on the next page

*p < .05 ** p < .01
Sources:
1 *Survey by Pew Research Center and Princeton Survey Research Associates, August 24–September 10, 2000.* Retrieved November 17, 2005 from the iPOLL Databank, The Roper Center for Public Opinion Research, University of Connecticut. Calculations based on the author's own analysis.

quality of schools, quality of health care, and treatment by the courts and police as whites. The issue is that a plurality or majority of whites believe that African Americans are just as well off as whites when it comes to access to health care, education, and types of jobs, while a plurality of African Americans believe they are a lot worse off than whites when it comes income, access to health care, education, and types of jobs. Most white respondents admit that African Americans face discrimination and that there are still major problems facing racial minorities, but this does not seem to affect their view that African Americans have about the same opportunities in life as they do themselves.

African Americans were more likely than whites to say that they often or very often experienced injustice because of their social background. While 4% of whites often or very often experience this injustice, 22% of African Americans claimed to often or very often experience this type of injustice. Two percent of whites but 38% of African Americans say they have experienced injustice because of their race or ethnic background. African Americans are more

Table 3.19. Continued

Why are people poor in your country?

How often is prejudice and discrimination against certain groups a reason for why there are poor people today?[2]

	Whites	African Americans	χ^2	Cramer's V
			98.3**	.133**
Very often	9%	30%		
Often	24%	34%		
Sometimes	45%	26%		
Rarely	19%	6%		
Never	2%	3%		

How often is lack of equal opportunity a reason for why there are poor people today?[3]

	Whites	African Americans	χ^2	Cramer's V
			70.3**	.113**
Very often	8%	22%		
Often	23%	37%		
Sometimes	42%	30%		
Rarely	24%	10%		
Never	3%	2%		

Continued on next page

*p < .05 ** p < .01
Sources:
2–3 *Data from the International Social Justice Project (ISJP), International Social Justice Project 1991 [Computer file]. Ann Arbor, MI: Duane F. Alwin, David M. Klingel, and Merilynn Dielman, University of Michigan, Institute for Social Research, Program in Socio-Environmental Studies [producers], 1993.* Ann Arbor, MI: Inter-university Consortium for Political and Social Research. Calculations based on the author's own analysis.

likely than whites to say that they often or very often experience injustice because of a lack of money. Twelve percent of whites and 32% of African Americans say they have experienced injustice because of a lack of money.[4]

There is a solid relationship between race and the belief that discrimination is a reason for poverty. Only 33% of whites but 65% of African Americans believe that discrimination is often or very often a reason for poverty. There is also a difference in the perceived effect of moral fortitude, 41% of whites but 59% of

Table 3.19. Continued

Why are people poor in your country?

How often is each of the following factors a reason for why there are rich people in this country today? Dishonesty?[4]

	Whites	African Americans	χ^2	Cramer's V
			36.2**	.081**
Very often	16%	30%		
Often	25%	30%		
Sometimes	39%	25%		
Rarely	19%	14%		
Never	<1%	2%		

*p < .05 ** p < .01

Sources:

4 *Data from the International Social Justice Project (ISJP), International Social Justice Project 1991 [Computer file]. Ann Arbor, MI: Duane F. Alwin, David M. Klingel, and Merilynn Dielman, University of Michigan, Institute for Social Research, Program in Socio-Environmental Studies [producers], 1993.* Ann Arbor, MI: Inter-university Consortium for Political and Social Research. Calculations based on the author's own analysis.

African Americans believe that dishonesty is often or very often a reason for being rich. In addition, 31% of whites but 59% of African Americans believe that lack of equal opportunity is a cause of poverty. This suggests that African Americans may have a different definition of equal opportunity. Whites may view equal opportunity in political terms, while African Americans view it economically. It could also be that African Americans also view it politically, but believe that legal restrictions still exist or that current laws have not really eliminated barriers. Whatever the case may be, African Americans and whites do disagree on several issues.

Conclusions

Bill Clinton's statement at the beginning of the chapter effectively summarizes an ideal that is a central tenet of the meritocratic ethos. Americans tend to believe that people have equal opportunities to get ahead, that they get rewarded for their effort, and that people get rewarded for their intelligence and skill. But Americans are also a realistic group of people. Many Americans know that one's race, social background, and connections matter for success. This is a direct violation of the meritocratic ideal. Unfortunately, there is insufficient data to discern whether Americans are cognizant of these contradictory ideas. Previous research suggests that it is probably quite common for people not to "put two and two together" especially given the complex nature of the debate over meritocracy. There is certainly a lack of "ideological constraint" among the mass public on these issues. The key item for researchers to understand is that support for the meritocratic ethic is not absolute. The American creed might include items that make it difficult for smart, hardworking people to succeed solely by their own volition.

Overall, there is an interesting mix of results. The public displays a preference for the use of both merit and non-merit factors when making decisions regarding the allocation of economic resources. They believe that smart, hardworking people deserve higher pay, but are not convinced that those who have attained a prominent position in our economy have done so strictly through hard work. Most Americans believe that the disadvantaged should be given extra help and are willing to support programs that provide opportunities effectively. But they also believe that everyone has already had an equal opportunity and may view the programs as unnecessary. American culture values freedom and the family, therefore it is not surprising that Americans believe that wealthier people should be free to help their own children. This occurs, however, at the expense of meritocracy.

Notes

1. quoted in Hochschild 1995, 18

2. *Data from the International Social Justice Project (ISJP), International Social Justice Project 1991 [Computer file]. Ann Arbor, MI: Duane F. Alwin, David M. Klingel, and Merilynn Dielman, University of Michigan, Institute for Social Research, Program in Socio-Environmental Studies [producers], 1993.* Ann Arbor, MI: Inter-university Consortium for Political and Social Research. Calculations based on the author's own analysis. Margin of Error +/- 3%

3. *Data from the International Social Justice Project (ISJP), International Social Justice Project 1991 [Computer file]. Ann Arbor, MI: Duane F. Alwin, David M. Klingel, and Merilynn Dielman, University of Michigan, Institute for Social Research, Program in Socio-Environmental Studies [producers], 1993.* Ann Arbor, MI: Inter-university Consortium for Political and Social Research. Calculations based on the author's own analysis. Margin of Error +/- 3%

4. *Data from the International Social Justice Project (ISJP), International Social Justice Project 1991 [Computer file]. Ann Arbor, MI: Duane F. Alwin, David M. Klingel, and Merilynn Dielman, University of Michigan, Institute for Social Research, Program in Socio-Environmental Studies [producers], 1993.* Ann Arbor, MI: Inter-university Consortium for Political and Social Research. Calculations based on the author's own analysis. Margin of Error +/- 3%

Chapter 4

Meritocracy Revealed: The Case of Inheritance and Its Taxation

I set out on this ground, which I suppose to be self-evident, that the earth belongs in usufruct to the living; that the dead have neither powers nor rights over it. The portion occupied by any individual ceases to be his when himself ceases to be, and reverts to the society.[1]

Thomas Jefferson

Thomas Jefferson was actively opposed not only to the hereditary distribution of political power but to the hereditary distribution of economic power as well. The sage who set forth our ideas about natural and inalienable rights specifically claimed that there was no natural right to oblige others regarding the use of one's land beyond one's own death. "For if he could" said Jefferson, "the lands would belong to the dead, and not to the living, which is the reverse of our principle" (Jefferson 1944, 488–89). For Jefferson, the notion that the dead have rights violated his sense of justice.

Specifically, Jefferson proposed a plan "by which every fibre would be eradicated of ancient or future aristocracy; and a foundation laid for a government truly republican" (Jefferson 1944, 51). He sought the elimination of the laws of entail, laws that require that accumulated wealth be transmitted to heirs, and the abolition of primogeniture, the principle that the oldest male should receive the bulk of one's inheritance. The plan would prevent the accumulation of wealth in select families and bring an end to "feudal and unnatural distinctions" between children. It was a part of his plan for equality that wealth not be transmitted to one's children in perpetuity. In this way, each generation would start from scratch, relying only on their own virtues and talents to succeed.

On this particular issue, Jefferson deviated a great deal from John Locke, the political theorist from which Jefferson borrowed the idea of natural rights. Locke believed that inheritance was a natural right because he believed it was a part of natural law that parents should provide for their children (Locke 1960, 207). Jefferson, on the other hand, viewed inheritance as a civil right. The distinction is simple: natural rights could not be abridged by the government, but civil rights were granted by the government and could be regulated or even eliminated.

The American courts would come to accept Jefferson's view and interpreted inheritance to be a civil instead of natural right. In the case *Eyre v. Jacob* (1858) the Virginia Supreme Court stated that right to property by descent was properly subject to legislative regulation. The legislature could create, amend, or repeal statutes related to the use of property upon the owner's death. It could even, if it chose, appropriate the property for public use. The US Supreme Court agreed with the Virginia Court and the positivist view of inheritance reigned for the next 130 years (Chester 1982). But a look at American society today reveals that we are a long way away from Jefferson's ideal. Inherited wealth has remained imbedded in American society, and one's social and economic origins significantly impact one's life course.

Wealth and Inheritance

Discussions about wealth and inheritance are far from straightforward. Economists make a distinction between inherited wealth and lifecycle wealth. Inherited wealth is wealth that is transmitted from one generation to the next, while lifecycle wealth is wealth that is accumulated during one's lifetime. The distinction seems pretty clear but, because the devil is in the details, there is a huge difference of opinion among economists over what percentage of wealth in America belongs in either category.

Estimates range from over 80% to under 20% for inherited wealth in America. The high figure of 80% is calculated by including *inter vivos* gifts, like college expenses, and by adding capitalized interest. Since spending, even exorbitantly, on one's child is not technically a bequest, many choose not to count *inter vivos* gifts in inheritance even though such spending adds to differences in opportunities and overall wealth. For most of the population, these gifts are rather small and therefore don't play a major role in overall wealth (Pestieau 2003; Wolff 2003). And even though the estate tax increases the reasons to give *inter vivos* gifts, most wealth transfers occur through bequests (Kopczuk & Slemrod 2003, 245). Therefore, *inter vivos* gifts only have small effect on these calculations.

The addition of capitalized interest, however, can create havoc on estimates of inherited wealth. For example, if a person received a $100 million inheritance at the age of fifty-five and did nothing except have that money invested in a manner that produced 7% annual growth, that person would have over $250 million twenty years later at the age of seventy-five. Including the capitalized interest gives one a much higher proportion of wealth that stems from inheritance. Excluding it, by claiming that the $150 million gain is lifecycle wealth, decreases the proportion of wealth that is inherited. In the latter case, the economist would argue that $100 million was inherited and an additional $150 million has been "earned" since the inheritance. If this person had no other wealth other than what was gained from the inheritance and subsequent interest, it would drop the proportion of wealth that is inherited for that person from 100% to below 40%.

Or, take a second example. Suppose a young college graduate begins his career $50,000 in debt because of student loans and is paying interest on those loans for the standard ten years it takes to finish paying them; while a second student has the same expense paid for by his parents. The second has a positive figure of wealth accumulation right from the very beginning and is increasing his wealth at a much faster rate than the first graduate even if their incomes and expenses are identical after graduation. Whether we count this as inherited or lifecycle wealth makes a big difference in the percentage of total wealth that has today been inherited. Fortunately, other aspects of this debate are more clear-cut.

America is the wealthiest nation on earth and necessity requires that all the wealth must at some point be left behind and passed on to the next generation. The best estimates are that gifts and bequests account for approximately half of the total wealth in America (Munnell & Sundén 2003, 3). But this wealth is in the hands of a relatively small group. The top 1% owns over 38% of the wealth and the top 20% owns over 83% of the total wealth (McNamee & Miller 2004). Only a small proportion of households give or receive bequests in any given year and the vast majority of those are among the highest wealth holders (Menchik & Jianakoplos 1998). Only 20% of Americans ever receive a bequest in their lifetimes and only 2% of estates were large enough to be subject to the estate tax in 1998. In that year an estate must have been valued at over $600,000 to be subject to the tax (McNamee & Miller 2004).

These figures might be surprising to many Americans because households are too optimistic about how much they will leave as bequests; most use a significant portion to sustain themselves in old age (Mitchell 2003). Nevertheless, inheritance has a dramatic impact on individuals in society. According to McNamee and Miller, "Inheritance provides . . . prestigious cultural capital, economic help at critical junctures in the life course, insulation against downward mobility in the event of personal setbacks, as well as lump-sum estates upon the death of family members" (McNamee & Miller 2004, 193). These three items, cultural capital, assistance in the form of subsidies, and direct economic transfers, are transmitted from one generation to the next and have a significant impact on the child's life course.

Cultural capital, the skills of social interaction, linguistic styles, aesthetic tastes, and cultural codes of conduct that define one's social status are learned early in life. They are transferred to children from parents, other relatives, and acquaintances when the child is learning to socially interact with others. Often these skills can prevent otherwise bright individuals from ascending the social ladder (Miller & McNamee 1998). For example, a child who has experiences with adults at "beer and nachos" gatherings may one day feel the effects of his upbringing if he finds himself at a "wine and cheese" party as an adult. While these types of awkward social situations provide comic relief when portrayed on television and in movies, in reality the subtle norms of engagement act as a real barrier to the uninitiated.

Assistance in the form of subsidies comes in many forms, the most important of which is the provision of educational opportunities. We are told that education is the key to moving up in the world and educational attainment does have an independent effect on economic status (Brittain 1977). But because access to different types and quality of schooling are stratified, the resources of the parents have an important effect on the education a child will receive (Kerckhoff 1993). Upper-class individuals tend to receive the best educations while middle-class individuals receive mediocre educations. This impacts a child's future place in society. Those who inherit large estates also tend to have higher than average levels of human capital and education, thereby increasing their lifecycle earnings. This compounds the effect of having wealthy parents. The child receives money directly through bequest, but also earns more money on his own than those who don't receive bequests (De Nardi 1999). This phenomenon reinforces the *status quo* and makes social mobility difficult.

Finally, there is the direct transmission of economic resources in the form of *inter vivos* gifts and bequests (Miller & McNamee 1998). Intergenerational links are vital in understanding the emergence of large estates that are most often accumulated in multiple generations, especially in the upper tail of the wealth distribution (De Nardi 1999). In modern day America, economic status is largely explained by parental economic status. Indeed, most people remain in the same social class in which they were born. Those that do happen to move up or down the socio-economic status ladder tend to move a single place, for example from working class to middle class, rather than taking giant leaps up or down (Brittain 1977; Kerckhoff 1993; McNamee & Miller 2004).

This combination of cultural capital, subsidized education, and direct bequests leads to an ever-expanding gap between the rich and the poor. The wealth held by the top 1% grew dramatically between 1983 and 1998, while living conditions for the average American stagnated (Wolff 2003, 351). McNamee and Miller state that, "The really big money in America comes not from wages and salaries but from owning property—particularly the kind of property that produces more wealth" (McNamee & Miller 2004, 53–54). Once the wealth is accumulated it can be put into trust funds whereby descendants receive interest income "without digging into the principle fund" (McNamee & Miller 2004, 62). In terms of acquiring wealth, the cards are stacked against those who have very little to start with. Indeed, "Inheritance is as unrelated to effort and ability as is welfare, and it is usually unrelated to absolute need" (Chester 1982, 188). Generation after generation can live off the interest and still get richer without doing anything at all.

Americans love the myth of the self-made man, but the evidence overwhelmingly suggests that wealth ownership is highly stable over long periods.

Every year *Forbes* magazine publishes a list of the 400 wealthiest Americans. The majority of the people on that list inherited sums of over $50 million. Most of the wealthiest people in America were born that way and the same is true for the poorest Americans. According to one estimate, "95% of children born to parents in the bottom 6% of wealth holders will end up poor as adults" (McNamee & Miller 2004, 56). Because "the position of each person in the social structure depends upon the position of the family into which he is born," America "is properly classified as a caste society" (Lasswell 1976, 209).

Social mobility is rare in the US; where you start largely determines where you end up. In America,

> A common metaphor for the competition to get ahead in life is the footrace. . . . In this intergenerational relay race, children born to wealthy parents start at or near the finish line, while children born into poverty start behind everyone else. Those who are born close to the finish line do not need any merit to get ahead. They are already ahead. The poorest of the poor, however, need to traverse the entire distance to get to the finish line on the basis of merit alone. . . . Barring parental disinheritance, there is no realistic scenario in which they [the rich] end up destitute—regardless of the extent of their innate talent or individual motivation. Their future is financially secure. They will grow up having the best of everything and having every opportunity money can buy. . . . Despite the ideology of meritocracy, the reality in America as elsewhere is inheritance first and merit second (McNamee & Miller 2004, 49–51).

In order to put this wealth gap into perspective, a person would have to save, from their wages, nearly $120,000 every month for thirty-five years in order to accumulate $50 million. At the upper end of the wealth distribution, the money does not come from salaries and wages. Inheritance plays a much larger role in our lives than we might like to admit. It is therefore appropriate to ask whether inheritance is fair.

The Justice of Inheritance

In this regard, the justification for inheritance has changed as society has changed. As feudalism was replaced by modern liberal society, the notion of inheritance as an individual legal right replaced the feudal justifications for inheritance (Chester 1982, 11). Locke's natural rights argument supporting inheritance quickly lost out to ideas presented by the utilitarians, who rejected the concept of natural rights and strongly favored the taxation of inherited wealth in order to prevent the extraordinary accumulation of property among a small minority (Johnson & Eller 1998). J.S. Mill thought that a person should have the power to distribute his property by will as he saw fit, but also believed there should be limits on how much a person could acquire by such means. Since such bequests were merely the favor of others and did not require the use of one's own faculties, the government had a right to regulate and tax such transfers. He believed that those who wanted more than what they had inherited should have to work for it (Chester 1982, 29). Once the philosophical foundation existed for the rejection of inheritance as a natural right, legal theorists like William Blackstone were able to argue that the right to hold property ceases at death. This philosophical milestone occurred a full twenty years before Jefferson made the same claim (Chester 1982, 19). Since then, most of the normative literature has been critical of inheritance.

As socialism became popularized in the nineteenth century, arguments against inheritance became especially harsh. One socialist author boldly proclaimed, "[A]s a friend of mankind I am only interested in showing you that the privilege of securing money without earning it is morally wrong and must be destroyed" (Read 1918, xxv). Socialists claimed that there was a battle between laborers and capitalists and that as long as those who inherit wealth continued to do so generation after generation, there would be no way in which those who produce the wealth could acquire it. It was the workers who produced the wealth, but it was the owner's children who were reaping the rewards. For them, this was a fundamental violation of one's natural rights. They turned Locke's natural rights argument on its head and, like Jefferson, claimed that it was an injustice for those that are long dead to have a say in how the yet to be born will live their lives (Read 1918).

The socialists of that era believed that money acquired during one's lifetime should suffer little or no tax, while money acquired through inheritance should be taxed heavily. Specifically, assets acquired from one's father should be taxed at 50% and from one's grandfather, through one's father, at up to 100%. In this way, over the course of several generations all inherited wealth would revert to the state and advance the socialist project without violent or abrupt upheaval (Rignano 1924).

Even Adam Smith, the father of modern capitalism, was ambivalent with regard to inheritance. He believed it should be taxed if it was found that the well being of the majority could be enhanced by limiting the fortunes of heirs. But he also believed that diminishing large pools of capital would make it more difficult to maintain productive labor (Chester 1982, 21). A capitalist economy needs large pools of capital that can be invested in various pursuits, but it is not absolutely necessary that this capital be owned by a small select group nor that it be transmitted from parent to child. Capitalism does not require the christening of millionaires at birth. In practical terms, as long as Bill Gates' fortune remains invested in Microsoft, there is no capitalist requirement that his shares be given to his children or that they should receive dividend income after their father's death. As long as the capital remains invested and there is someone to manage it, it could belong to anyone or everyone without economic catastrophe.

Not all opposition to inheritance comes from egalitarian motives, however. Some comes from the meritocratic ideal that individuals should be rewarded for their hard work. From this perspective emerges the view that inheritances act as an incentive for indolence. In this regard, "Many conservatives become highly indignant at the prospect of poor people losing their incentives to work by being given welfare, yet these same conservatives are perfectly content with the prospect of rich people losing their incentives to work by being given large inheritances" (Haslett 1997, 140). It is believed that those who inherit large fortunes simply do not feel the necessity of working. The American conservative therefore finds himself contradicting his own values with regard to the wealthy.

Most of the arguments against limiting inheritances have been practical rather than philosophical or theoretical. The most popular seems to be that the estate tax constitutes double taxation because the accumulated wealth was already taxed when it was income. It is also argued that because of multiple tax avoidance schemes the actual revenue from inheritance taxes is minimal while the cost of these schemes in lawyer and accounting fees is significant. It's claimed that the administrative costs are especially high because assets must be valued for a "non-market" exchange. Because of these high costs, the opponents claim the tax is a waste of resources given that so little is gained by the fisc from the tax (Bracewell-Milnes 2002; Johnson & Eller 1998).

Some economists argue that the tax artificially shortens the time horizons by which investors calculate their decisions, thereby decreasing long-term investments and savings. Additionally, it is claimed that the tax decreases the amount of money available for investment and that it hurts small business owners and farmers who have a large proportion of their equity in non-liquid assets. Finally, some argue that the treasury loses money because, had the money remained saved or invested, it could have been collected later through a variety of other taxes (Bracewell-Milnes 2002; Johnson & Eller 1998).

Each of these practical considerations has been countered by proponents of the estate tax. The double taxation argument is specious for two reasons. The first is that it is not necessarily true that a decedent's acquired property has ever been taxed. If one's property is in the form of stocks and the stock increases in value, then one doesn't pay a tax until the stock is actually sold. If the stock is not sold within one's lifetime, then the increased value of the stock has never been subject to a tax. If one's property is in the form of government bonds, then one does not pay a tax on the earned interest. Indeed, part of the incentive for purchasing a government bond is the tax-free nature of the revenues from it. In both of these cases a person gets wealthier, but never pays a tax on their newfound wealth ("The Estate Tax").

Of course, if one's wealth comes strictly from wages, then paying an estate tax would constitute a double tax. We already noted that most wealth does not come from wages and salaries, but for the small proportion that is, simply stating that it's taxed twice does not make it *ipso facto* unjust. Individuals pay an income tax and then pay a sales tax when they buy consumer products or a utility tax when they pay their bills. Americans are told that they should carpool and limit unnecessary driving because it is good for the environment. This is the justification for taxes on the purchase of automobiles, taxes on the purchase of fuel for those automobiles, and fees for licensing and registering those automobiles. Americans are also told that smoking is harmful and costs hospitals lots of money and for those reasons cigarettes are subject to a sales tax and a tobacco tax. Many things, especially those things that we find socially harmful, are taxed two or three times without similar claims of injustice.

Some opponents of the estate tax argue that the administrative costs of the inheritance tax is high, while the actual revenues from it are low and use this as a justification for eliminating the tax altogether. Unfortunately, research shows that the cost of administering the tax is about 7% of total revenues. That is less than the administrative costs of the income tax ("The Estate Tax"). Of course, if one is concerned about insufficient revenues given the costs, then increasing the tax rate and decreasing the exemption amounts would increase revenues without increasing the administrative costs.

The argument that the inheritance tax artificially decreases the time horizon for a return on investments depends on one's perspective. How many people make an investment with an eye toward collecting their profit at some point beyond their own deaths? I suspect that most investors would like to see a return on their investment while they are still alive. Since death is a natural and unavoidable act, the ability to transfer property to heirs artificially elongates the time horizon for investments. What constitutes "artificial" shortening of a time perspective is clearly subjective.

Eliminating the estate tax would not necessarily lead to increased private savings, as opponents of the tax argue. Some people will choose to spend their inheritance and therefore it can't be claimed that eliminating the tax automatically increases the money available for investment. It is also factually untrue that the tax significantly harms family-owned businesses and farms. According to researchers, "[I]f the current exemption level of $1.5 million had been in place in 2000, only 300 farm estates and only 223 family-owned businesses nationwide would have owed any estate tax. The number of taxable farm estates drops to sixty-five nationwide at a $3.5 million exemption level, the level that takes effect in 2009. The number of taxable family-owned business estates falls to just ninety-four under the $3.5 million exemption" ("The Estate Tax"). Of the sixty-five farms that would be taxable "just thirteen would have faced liquidity constraints" ("The Estate Tax"). Only a tiny proportion of millionaire families would face the problem of having to sell off non-liquid assets. This is in part because section 6166 of the 1976 tax bill solved this problem decades ago (Johnson & Eller 1998). Furthermore, the majority of gross estates come from stocks and bonds, only 19% is in the form of real estate (Kopczuk & Slemrod 2003, 218).

Some arguments against the inheritance tax rest on a very peculiar assumption. Some opponents treat the donor just like any other existing economic actor who makes choices between competing uses. Bracewell-Milnes believes it is "beside the point" to talk about whether the person who receives the bequest is deserving because the donor is the active party (Bracewell-Milnes 2002, 38). "Ultimately," he argues the donor can choose "between spending and bequest" (Bracewell-Milnes 2002, 38). However, this assumption stands in direct opposition to Jeffersonian justice. It assumes that the property belongs to the dead and that the dead have rights over it. Given Jefferson's materialism and adherence to natural philosophy he might also point out a related flaw in the assumption. The dead, *ipso facto*, are incapable of making decisions between spending and bequesting. Although it is now cliché to say, "you can't take it with you," it is clear that the donor has no choice but to leave his property behind. The question at stake is whether the dead should be allowed to dictate what happens to their property, or even more fundamentally whether they are capable of ownership at all.

We could reasonably argue that while alive the now deceased donor preferred keeping the property rather than spending it. This argument rests on the notion that the donor preferred potential over actual use and might be closer to what Bracewell-Milnes actually meant. However, if the donor simply enjoyed saving for the sake of saving, then even a 100% estate tax would have no effect on his lifetime savings to be left behind. And, so long as the person can keep saving while they are alive, they lose no utility from the loss of their savings upon death. In the end, the only way to hold firm to Bracewell-Milnes' justification would be to add the question "what would make the dead happy" into our social utility function.

In this debate, we begin to see that proponents and opponents of the estate tax disagree on a fundamental question. They disagree on whether the deceased or the heir is the subject of the tax. The opponents argue that the decedent has a right to distribute his money as he sees fit, without government taxation. The proponents argue that the heir does not deserve the wealth because he has not worked for it and that the institution of inheritance itself causes an increase in inequality and low rates of social mobility for the talented and hardworking. Many of these arguments about the justness of inheritance and its taxation have been raised every time a change in the policy has been proposed.

The History of Inheritance Taxation

The taxation of property upon one's death has existed since ancient times. Both the ancient Egyptians and Romans imposed duties on the transferring of property due to the death of the property holder (Johnson & Eller 1998). However, the custom of inheritance comes to us more directly from the European feudal tradition (Chester 1982). Between 1600 and 1800 the purpose of bequests was to "maximize the wealth and power of the eldest male head of the lineage" and bequests were "not considered distasteful" (Delong 2003, 34). Because of shorter life spans and slower rates of economic growth inheritances made up approximately 90% of wealth acquisition before the industrial revolution. Today that figure stands at about 45% (Delong 2003).

The reason primogeniture became standard practice was twofold. First, fiefdoms were granted only to individuals. It made sense to replace one fief with another by succession from father to eldest son. This would ensure continuity of the feudal hierarchy and maintain social stability. Secondly, the "divided we fall" argument also favored primogeniture. Divided lands were more easily conquered, therefore maintaining the integrity of a large estate was essential for security. Together these two reasons are known as the "feudal-military" rationale for primogeniture. The majority of wealth holdings at that time came from bequests, and primogeniture remained in England even after the "feudal-military" rationale no longer applied. The newly rich sought to emulate the norms of the landed aristocracy and maintained primogeniture as a method of enhancing the status of the lineage (Delong 2003).

However, in nineteenth-century America primogeniture was replaced with the idea that wealth should be distributed equally to one's children. For one, it may have been difficult to get a younger son to work the land if he knows he will inherit none of it, especially when he can leave to work his own land on the western frontier. We were also entering the Industrial Revolution and with it came the idea that upward mobility is a social virtue. Those who have worked for their riches were seen as more deserving and the status claims of inherited wealth declined. By the end of the twentieth century, disapproval of inheritances was symbolized by a permanent estate tax. The repeal of the estate tax could be seen as a new shift in thinking, and inheritances may once again be viewed a legitimate means of acquiring wealth (Delong 2003).

Early forms of the inheritance tax in the US were temporary solutions to financial crises. The first inheritance tax in the US was the Stamp Tax of 1797, which required federal stamps on wills, inventories, letters of administration, and on receipts and discharges from legacies. The tax was imposed to raise funds for the financing of our naval hostilities with France. However, once the hostilities were over in 1802 the tax was repealed. The Civil War again required that the federal government raise revenues and a new inheritance tax was created in 1862. In addition to a document tax on wills, this new tax also included taxes on the property itself and on *inter vivos* gifts. Like future transfer taxes, the 1862 law exempted widows and very small estates. But it too was repealed in 1870 after the Civil War ended and the additional revenues became unnecessary (Johnson & Eller 1998).

The Industrial Revolution saw the amassing of great fortunes and growing concern about economic inequality. Andrew Carnegie, a wealthy industrialist himself, believed that leaving great amounts of wealth to one's children destroyed their will to develop and use their talents and ultimately cost society. He believed that the wealth should be used for the public benefit. This, along with the popular idea that people should work for what they have, ultimately led to the modern inheritance tax in 1916. Teddy Roosevelt supported the tax because "he thought that huge inherited fortunes would ruin the character of the republic" ("Ever Higher Society"). Since then, most of the changes were relatively minor, for example, changes in tax rates or exclusion amounts (Johnson & Eller 1998). The National Tax Association Conference in 1924 argued for light taxes on income from a person's own effort and heavy taxes on income from inheritances. Their proposed program would not penalize initiative and reduce the passing on of large fortunes across generations (Chester 1982, 71).

In the 1970s and 1980s several loopholes were closed in the inheritance tax system. The first was the addition of a "generation skipping transfer (GST)" tax. This was an additional tax imposed on transfers made to grandchildren. Since it was possible to avoid paying a generation's worth of estate taxes by skipping generations, the GST tax eliminated the problem. It was also possible to pay fewer taxes through *inter vivos* gifts, so the gift tax and estate tax were combined into a single system to prevent lost revenue from estate gifts while a person was still alive (Johnson & Eller 1998).

In 1987, however, the US Supreme Court seems to have broken with over a century's worth of precedent in *Hodel v. Irving*. The Indian Land Consolidation Act of 1983 declared that parcels of land that were too small to be economical could be forfeited to the tribe upon a tribe members death, this would stop the excessive fragmentation of land holdings that had become a problem over the course of several generations. The Court declared that this act was unconstitutional because the right to pass on property at death was constitutionally protected, but it left the legislature's ability to regulate the transfer of that property intact. The case is therefore ambiguous in terms of its ultimate effect on inheritance jurisprudence, but it may pave the way for a natural rights interpretation of inheritance in the years to come (Chester 1982).

Today, there are still those wealthy Americans who value merit and who place a priority on the value of hard work. Both Bill Gates and Warren Buffet plan on leaving the bulk of their estates to private charities, reserving only small amounts for their heirs. Jamie Johnson, heir of the Johnson & Johnson pharmaceuticals fortune, realizes that he will never have to work for a living. But he is using his resources to finance a career as a documentary filmmaker who focuses on exposing the world of the super rich. His friends, like himself, are inheritors of hundreds of millions, even billions of dollars. Johnson accepts the unmeritocratic nature of his station in life, but has chosen to make it visible to the mass public (*Born Rich* 2004). These examples are noteworthy precisely because they are the exception to the rule. Like most Americans, most wealthy Americans ignore or reject meritocratic norms when it comes to inheritance.

The Estate Tax

Beginning in the 1990s several House and Senate bills were proposed to eliminate the estate, gift, and GST tax. In addition, Bob Dole vowed to eliminate the estate tax for family businesses and farms during his presidential campaign (Johnson & Eller 1998). George W. Bush made similar promises during his 2000 presidential campaign and the federal estate tax is now scheduled to be phased out as part of President Bush's tax relief plan of 2001. Before the reform the estate tax only applied to estates valued at over $1 million. Starting in 2006 it only applied to estates valued at over $2 million. Then in 2009 it will only apply to estates valued at $3.5 million or more. The figures are doubled for couples, i.e., $7 million exempt in 2009. It would be completely abolished in 2010 only to return to pre-reform levels in 2011. However, there have been several attempts in Congress to make the repeal permanent. The yearly tax-free gift allowed has been increased to $11,000 with a lifetime exclusion limit of $1 million.

The estate tax only affects the very rich and at its peak only affected 6% of decedents (Kopczuk & Slemrod 2003). Typically, less than 2% of deaths are required to pay estate taxes in any given year (Johnson & Eller 1998). These taxes only affect the top 1% of estates and most of those pay less than 20% in taxes, even though the maximum tax rate is 50%. This is because of the very high initial exemption levels. The top tax rate itself will decline to 45% by 2009 ("The Estate Tax"). There are also several mechanisms by which one can reduce or eliminate paying the tax. Bequests to spouses and charities are tax-free and deductions are allowed for debts, final expenses, state estate taxes, and legal fees associated with the estate (Kopczuk & Slemrod 2003).

Despite the small numbers of those affected, there would be serious social repercussions if the tax were eliminated. Analysts have predicted that permanent repeal would cost the government over $1 trillion dollars over the first ten years and that many programs would need to be cut or deficits increased to make up for the lost revenues ("The Estate Tax"). The estate tax also reduces the accumulation of large estates by the wealthy by 10.5%, suggesting the tax is effective at reducing wealth inequality (Kopczuk & Slemrod 2003, 245). And because charitable contributions are deductible from the taxable estate, the tax has the effect of increasing charitable giving by 12%. Ultimately, reducing or eliminating the estate tax will lead to fewer charitable contributions (Kopczuk & Slemrod 2003, 227).

Economists and policy analysts have often tried to determine people's motivations for leaving a bequest. Motives are important because they may influence bequests given certain policies. For example, if bequests are accidental or if individuals accumulate wealth simply because they get pleasure from holding it, then changes in the estate tax won't make a difference. If, however, the motive is altruistic, then increasing the estate tax may discourage savings for the purpose of bequests (Gale & Potter 2003).

To date, there has been a great deal of speculation regarding the motives people have for leaving bequests. The most common rationale is that individuals accumulate wealth in case of poor health later in life and if any remains upon their death it is left as a bequest (Orzag 2003). Indeed, data from retired Americans shows that those with children and those without decumulate their wealth at the same rate, suggesting there no bequest motive (Hurd 2003). Others argue that bequests are used to influence the behavior of benefactors, compelling certain behaviors and discouraging others (Andreoni 2003). Proponents of "identification theory" believe that people give money to those they identify with, especially family and friends, but also charities (Shervish & Havens 2003). Finally, some believe that wealth is an end in itself and that people get pleasure from simply having it. This suggests that bequests are accidental byproducts of self-interested behavior (Diamond 2003).

Inheritances and Public Opinion

Whereas in many areas of distributive preferences we see a substantial but not entirely meritocratic set of values, in the specific case of inheritances and estate taxes Americans are resolutely unmeritocratic. Eighty-four percent of Americans strongly agree with the statement that people are entitled to pass on their wealth to their children. As a question of individual rights, Americans seem to directly conflict with the view presented by Jefferson regarding the fairness of inherited economic power. This view also directly conflicts with the ideals of meritocratic justice.

Even in the distribution of inheritances themselves are Americans unmeritocratic. A majority of heads of households believe that all children should receive the same amount. Only 24% believe bequests should be given according to need and 17% according to merit. Additionally, likely voters tend not be convinced by the argument that repealing the estate tax would create a two-tiered society where some people become rich through inherited wealth instead of hard work. Arguing that inheritances cause some people to become rich through nonwork is not a powerful motivator against eliminating the estate tax. When pitting the value of hard work against the rights of decedents, hard work seems to lose out.

Part of what makes deciphering public opinion difficult on the question of the estate tax is the visceral reaction against taxes in general. It seems that simply using the word "tax" creates negative feelings and causes people to oppose anything with the word tax in it. We can be fairly certain that the question, "Would you like the government to eliminate the _____ tax?" will be answered with a resounding "Yes!" regardless of what tax we're talking about. We can

Table 4.1. Inheritances, Merit, and Hard Work

People are entitled to pass on their wealth to their children.[1]

Strongly agree	84%
Somewhat agree	15%
Neither agree or disagree	<1%
Somewhat disagree	<1%
Strongly disagree	<1%

In planning their estate, should parents give to their children equally, according to their needs, or according to individual merit?[2]

Equally	54%
According to needs	24%
According to individual merit	17%
Not sure	5%

Continued on the next page

Sources:
1 *Data from the International Social Justice Project (ISJP), International Social Justice Project 1991 [Computer file]. Ann Arbor, MI: Duane F. Alwin, David M. Klingel, and Merilynn Dielman, University of Michigan, Institute for Social Research, Program in Socio-Environmental Studies [producers], 1993.* Ann Arbor, MI: Inter-university Consortium for Political and Social Research. Calculations based on the author's own analysis. Margin of Error +/- 2%
2 *Survey by Lutheran Brotherhood, conducted by Louis Harris & Associates, July 27–August 8, 1993.* Retrieved March 15, 2005 from the iPOLL Databank, The Roper Center for Public Opinion Research, University of Connecticut.

expect opposition to the estate tax, simply because it is a tax and not because most people are affected by it. Indeed, a majority of voters favor eliminating the inheritance tax and approved of a congressional tax plan that included a cut in the inheritance tax. Even after being told that the estate tax only affects millionaires, a 60% majority of Americans still favored its elimination. Astoundingly, a 43% plurality realize that they will not personally benefit from the repeal of the estate tax and 39% "Don't know enough to say."

Can it be that almost 40% of the population is holding out for the possibility that they may have some yet unknown millionaire relative that is going to pick them for some lump sum payment upon their death? No, most Americans do not expect to receive an inheritance. Fully 60% of non-retired people say that inhe-

Table 4.1. Continued

Now, as I said before, Congress is now considering legislation to eliminate the estate tax. Some people are opposed to this legislation. I am going to read you some reasons these people give to oppose this legislation. Please rate each reason on a scale of 0 to 10 with 10 meaning it is an extremely convincing reason to oppose this legislation, 0 meaning it is a totally unconvincing reason to oppose this legislation, and 5 meaning it is neither convincing nor unconvincing. America is founded on the notion of equal opportunity for all. Eliminating the estate tax creates a two-tiered society where some individuals do better than others based on inherited wealth rather than hard work.[3]
Mean = 4.6

0—4 Unconvincing	37%
5 Neither convincing nor unconvincing	28%
6	5%
7	5%
8	5%
9	3%
10—Extremely convincing	13%
Don't know	4%

Source:
3 *Survey conducted by Greenberg Quinlan Rosner Research, May 6–May 9, 2002.* Retrieved March 15, 2005 from the iPOLL Databank, The Roper Center for Public Opinion Research, University of Connecticut.

ritance will not be a source of income for them when they retire and 85% of those that are retired say it is not presently a source of income. Only 8% say they have received a bequest in the past five years,[2] and only 12% have had or expect to receive a large inheritance.[3] Because most bequests are small, a majority of those who have received a bequest in the past five years claim that it had no effect on their savings, suggesting that whatever money was received was immediately spent.[4] The preference for eliminating the estate tax does not come from a belief that one will personally gain a large sum of money from the death of an ancestor.

The question in the preceding paragraph was facetious, of course, but Americans' optimism is entirely unrealistic. The only other conclusion is that they expect to one day be millionaires and therefore believe that they may benefit from the repeal of the estate tax in the future. With some certainty, we can say that 39% of Americans are not going to become wealthy within the next few decades. To be fair, a majority of Americans realize they will not be rich. The reason that many Americans believe they may one day benefit from the estate tax repeal is because slightly over 40% believe there is some likelihood that they will become wealthy.

A Gallup survey, which included a third option to repeal estate taxes only on small business and family farms, found a plurality favoring a repeal of all estate taxes and a minority favoring leaving all estate taxes in place. Most of this difference seems to come from those who otherwise favored leaving the tax in place. This suggests that Americans sympathize with "not really rich" wealth holders. Farmers and small business owners sometimes face hardships despite having relatively large amounts of invested capital. People who think the estates

Table 4.2. Support for Eliminating the Estate Tax

Which of the following types of taxes, if any, do you think should be reduced? As I read each one, please tell me if you think it should be reduced or not.[1]
Note: Adds to more than 100% due to multiple responses

The income tax	68%
The inheritance tax or "death tax"	62%
The higher tax on married couples	72%
The capital gains tax	47%
All taxes in general	60%
None of the above	4%

I'd like your opinion of some programs and proposals being discussed in this country today. Please tell me if you strongly favor, favor, oppose, or strongly oppose each one. Eliminating the inheritance tax.[2]
Note: Registered voters

Strongly favor	43%
Favor	28%
Oppose	15%
Strongly oppose	8%

Continued on the next page

Sources:
1 *Survey by Investor's Business Daily, Christian Science Monitor, conducted by TIPP-Techno Metrica Institute of Policy and Politics, February 8–February 12, 2001.* Retrieved March 15, 2005 from the iPOLL Databank, The Roper Center for Public Opinion Research, University of Connecticut.
2 *Survey by Pew Research Center, conducted by Princeton Survey Research Associates, August 24–September 10, 2000.* Retrieved March 15, 2005 from the iPOLL Databank, The Roper Center for Public Opinion Research, University of Connecticut.

Table 4.2. Continued

As you may or may not know, Congress recently passed a tax cut that reduces income tax rates by as much as 7%, cuts the marriage penalty, cuts inheritance taxes, and reduces taxes on what is commonly called capital gains—which are profits made from investments, selling of a home, or other capital items. Do you approve or disapprove of this tax cut?[3]

Strongly approve	39%
Somewhat approve	29%
Somewhat disapprove	14%
Strongly disapprove	17%

I would like to ask you a couple of questions about taxes that are paid on money or assets which are inherited when someone dies. As you may know, federal inheritance taxes currently apply to estates valued at more than $1 million. A new proposal would eliminate all inheritance taxes on estates over $1 million as well. Would you favor or oppose that proposal?[4]

Favor	60%
Oppose	35%
No opinion	5%

Continued on the next page

Sources:
3 *Survey conducted by Wirthlin Worldwide, August 6–August 9, 1999.* Retrieved March 15, 2005 from the iPOLL Databank, The Roper Center for Public Opinion Research, University of Connecticut.
4 *Survey by Cable News Network, USA Today, conducted by Gallup Organization, June 22–June 25, 2000.* Retrieved March 15, 2005 from the iPOLL Databank, The Roper Center for Public Opinion Research, University of Connecticut.

of the wealthy should be taxed have a specific vision in mind when they decide who should be subject to additional taxes. The combination of strong anti-tax sentiment in general, unrealistic optimism, and sympathy for small business owners and farmers produces a strong majority favoring the repeal of the estate tax when it is mentioned in a vacuum.

After being given a list of ten reasons to oppose the elimination of the inheritance tax and asked if each of the arguments was convincing, likely voters were asked the standard vacuum type question, "Do you favor or oppose legislation to eliminate the estate tax?" Rather than favoring its elimination, the public was now split.[5] How is that the enthusiasm for tax relief wanes from one survey question to the next? The answer is that each question evokes a different set of

Table 4.2. Continued

If such a proposal (that would eliminate all inheritance taxes on estates valued at more than $1 million) were passed into law, do you think you would or would not personally benefit from such a law in the future, or don't you know enough to say?[5]

Would personally benefit	17%
Would not personally benefit	43%
Don't know enough to say	39%
No opinion	1%

When you retire, how much do you expect to rely on each of the following sources of money? How about money from an inheritance?[6]
Note: Those non—retired

Major source	8%
Minor source	31%
Not at source	60%
No opinion	1%

How much do you rely on each of the following sources of income today? How about money from an inheritance?[7]
Note: Those retired

Major source	3%
Minor source	11%
Not a source	85%
No opinion	1%

Sources:
[5] *Survey by Cable News Network, USA Today, conducted by Gallup Organization, June 22–June 25, 2000.* Retrieved March 15, 2005 from the iPOLL Databank, The Roper Center for Public Opinion Research, University of Connecticut.
[6—7] *Survey conducted by Gallup Organization, April 5–April 8, 2004.* Retrieved March 15, 2005 from the iPOLL Databank, The Roper Center for Public Opinion Research, University of Connecticut.

considerations. When tax relief is proposed without any countervailing costs, of course it will be favored. However, after some thought on the matter support begins to decline. Public opinion regarding the estate tax is malleable, and other considerations can sway people who would normally favor the elimination of estate taxes to oppose the change.

When it came to the actual proposed plan that included a tax refund for middle-income families along with the elimination of the estate tax, voters were split.[6] There was not strong support for the plan, even though it included tangible benefits for many taxpayers. When cuts in education are placed in tandem with tax benefits for the wealthiest of Americans, the support falls to below majority levels. A refund of a few hundred dollars is not enough for most people to jump onto the anti-estate tax bandwagon when important programs and budget deficits are also considered.

The indecisiveness begins to swing toward the other end of the spectrum when people are confronted only with costs of the repeal of the estate tax. A majority of voters say they would be more likely to vote for a Democratic candidate for president if the candidate promised to maintain the estate tax.[7] That result is true when Americans are told that such taxes are used for social security and education and that the tax revenue comes from "unearned income." While Americans favor tax cuts in general, they don't favor a tax break for millionaires at the expense of favored programs.

This malleability stems in part from the low importance people place on the estate tax, from generally low levels of knowledge about the estate tax, and from distinctions made between work and non-work income. A majority of American investors regarded repealing the estate tax as a low priority. If voters had the ability to choose which taxes they would like to see reduced, a paltry 6% select to have the estate tax reduced. A plurality of Americans favor across-the-board tax relief. Income taxes are the preferred tax to reduce and, as in previous instances, a reduction in the estate tax ranks far below assistance with educating the young. Although voters were not convinced by the "children of rich people won't want to work hard" argument, they did find convincing the argument that it would be better to give tax breaks to the middle class and keep the estate tax in place.

A majority of Americans don't know if the inheritance tax is too high or too low. Because it is among the items that are not of major importance to most Americans, they are not very knowledgeable about it. Indeed, a plurality of voters say that if a congressman voted to eliminate the inheritance tax it would not impact their vote for that candidate. In accordance with the low priority voters place on estate tax relief, they believe that income from work should be taxed at a lower rate than income from non-work items such as dividends, interest, capital gains, and inheritance. Even though Americans believe that all taxes should be reduced, if they had to choose they would prefer to reduce those taxes that actually impact them. They prefer that their own personal income taxes would be reduced, or that they receive tax credits for educational expenses, rather than reducing the taxes on wealthy estate holders.

Economists have tried a variety of techniques to try to determine the reason why people leave bequests and there is no direct survey data on this subject. We do know that a majority of Americans believe it is important to save e-

Table 4.3. Explaining Support for Estate Tax Repeal

How likely is it that you will ever become wealthy, because of your work, investments, inheritance, or good luck?[1]

Very likely	12%
Somewhat likely	29%
Not too likely	31%
Not at all likely	26%
Already wealthy (vol.)	1%

I would like to ask you a couple of questions about taxes that are paid on money or assets which are inherited when someone dies. As you may know, federal inheritance taxes currently apply only to estates valued at more than $1 million. Which of the following would you prefer to see Congress do this year?[2]

Change the laws to eliminate all inheritance taxes on all estates	39%
Eliminate inheritance taxes on small businesses and family farms but otherwise leave the taxes unchanged	30%
Leave inheritance tax laws unchanged	25%

Sources:
1 *Survey by Newsweek, conducted by Princeton Survey Research Associates, June 24–June 25, 1999.* Retrieved March 15, 2005 from the iPOLL Databank, The Roper Center for Public Opinion Research, University of Connecticut.
2 *Survey conducted by Gallup Organization, February 19–February 21, 2001.* Retrieved March 15, 2005 from the iPOLL Databank, The Roper Center for Public Opinion Research, University of Connecticut.

nough money to leave an inheritance to their children[8] and that less than a quarter believe they will have nothing to leave,[9] suggesting that there is a real bequest motive that can only be implied by econometrics. However, a majority of Americans don't have a savings plan for the purpose of conferring an inheritance as an explicit investment goal.[10] This suggests that whatever is being left behind better conforms to the accidental model of bequests. Although Americans believe it is important to save enough to provide a bequest, most are not putting aside "untouchable" money for that purpose. It is not surprising then that most Americans fail to leave a bequest. Those that say they have specifically planned to leave a bequest have no set figure, but a plurality of those that do plan and have a set amount expect to give more than half a million dollars.[11] While most Americans think it's good to leave money behind for their children, only the very rich have a plan to actually do so and know exactly how much they are going to leave behind.

Discussion

At the founding of the American republic, hostility against the hereditary aristocracy extended not only to the political but to the economic realm as well. The injustice of hereditary monarchy was abolished in the new nation and attempts were made to abolish the transmission of wealth along family lines from one generation to the next. Inheritance was deemed a civil instead of a natural right and a foundation was laid for the future taxation of accumulated wealth upon the death of the owner.

Unfortunately, the Jeffersonian ideal was never realized. Wealth has a significant effect on how people live and where people end up in the social hierarchy. Those that are born to wealthy parents are born with easy access to the best opportunities available, while those born into poverty must struggle for survival. In the race to succeed, some people are born having already won, while others will finish behind regardless of their individual talents or efforts. In America today,

> inheritance and meritocracy coexist. Both factors operate in determining who gets what and how much. For the most part, however, meritocracy is superimposed on inheritance rather than the other way around. In other words, whatever effects produced by merit or luck or current life circumstances come *after* whatever effects are produced by the advantages (or disadvantages) of initial class placement at birth (McNamee & Miller 2004, 200).

Although inheritance plays a larger role in an individual's life course than their natural ability and hard work, the public has yet to fully accept the implications of that fact.

The arguments supporting inheritance have their roots in feudal Europe and natural law. But for most of the nineteenth and twentieth centuries these arguments lost to the egalitarian and meritocratic claims against their legitimacy. The estate tax has been a permanent feature of the American tax code for nearly a century and regular efforts were made to close loopholes while at the same time exempting those who were not wealthy. Despite these efforts, we have never achieved the meritocratic ideal.

The tax has always been levied only on the wealthiest Americans with the vast majority never being subject to the tax. Recently, however, the claims of this wealthy minority are being considered in the public discourse. The estate tax is being phased out and calls are being made for its permanent repeal

Table 4.4. Estate Tax is Low Priority

Now, I am going to read you a list of issues that the Congress and the President can address in the next session of Congress. For each one, please tell me if you think it should be one of the top priority issues the President and Congress should deal with, a major priority but not top priority, minor priority, or something the Congress should not deal with at all. How about repealing the federal tax on any inheritance?[1]
Note: Asked of investors

Top priority	17%
Major priority, but not top	29%
Minor priority	39%
President & Congress should not deal with it	12%

If there were going to be a tax cut in the next year, which of the following would be your priority for a tax cut?[2]

A tax cut for moderate and low income Americans	36%
A tax cut for all Americans	29%
Eliminating the marriage penalty	17%
A capital gains tax cut on real estate and stock sales	9%
An inheritance and estate tax cut	6%
Combination/Other (vol.)	2%

Continued on the next page

Sources:
1 *Survey by UBS, conducted by Gallup Organization, December 1–December 15, 2002.* Retrieved March 15, 2005 from the iPOLL Databank, The Roper Center for Public Opinion Research, University of Connecticut.
2 *Survey conducted by Greenberg Quinlan Rosner Research, May 6–May 9, 2002.* Retrieved March 15, 2005 from the iPOLL Databank, The Roper Center for Public Opinion Research, University of Connecticut.

by heirs and heiresses that claim they are being treated unjustly. Many have begun to wonder whether this new shift in thinking will re-legitimize inherited wealth as a just method of wealth acquisition.

The public seems to favor the natural rights interpretation that giving an inheritance to one's heirs is a liberty that should not be circumscribed or limited by the government. However, this view may stem in part from unrealistic optimism. Even though most Americans know they will never receive an inheritance, many believe that they may one day be able to leave one behind. The statistics

Table 4.4. Continued

If there were going to be a tax cut in the next year, which of the following would be your priority for a tax cut?[3]

Tax cut for moderate and low-income Americans	29%
Tax cut for all Americans	31%
Eliminating marriage penalty	15%
Capital gains tax cut	5%
Inheritance and estate tax cut	7%
Combination (vol.)	10%

If the government cuts taxes, which of the following taxes would you like to have cut first?[4]

Gas taxes	20%
Income taxes	42%
Property taxes	19%
Inheritance taxes	16%

Continued on the next page

Sources:
3 *Survey by NBC News, Wall Street Journal, conducted by Hart and Teeter Research Companies, January 13–January 15, 2000.* Retrieved March 15, 2005 from the iPOLL Databank, The Roper Center for Public Opinion Research, University of Connecticut.
4 *Survey by Fox News. Methodology, conducted by Opinion Dynamics, July 12–July 13, 2000.* Retrieved March 15, 2005 from the iPOLL Databank, The Roper Center for Public Opinion Research, University of Connecticut.

show that most will fail in their plan to leave a bequest, but when stated in a vacuum, most Americans still support the repeal of the estate tax.

If, however, the repeal of the estate tax is considered along with other items, then support for its elimination begins to wane. When they are told that the taxes are used for education and social security and that the tax comes from "unearned income," there is solid support for the tax. Indeed, eliminating the estate tax is a very low priority for most Americans. This is entirely rational since so few are affected by it. Rather than a cut in the estate tax, most Americans would rather see a cut in the income tax and other taxes that affect middle class taxpayers.

Interestingly, Americans are not swayed by the argument that the institution of inheritance creates a two-tiered society where some people are born rich without making any effort of their own while others struggle to get by despite working hard. Like in many policy areas, the way the issue is framed makes a

Table 4.4. Continued

The following are some tax cuts that are being considered by President (Bill) Clinton and Congress. Please tell me which one, if any, you would most like to see passed.[5]

Tax credit for college tuition	30%
Tax credit for families with young children	33%
Reduction in capital gains tax on sales of real estate or stock	20%
Reduction in estate or inheritance tax	12%
None of them (vol.)	2%

Congress is now considering legislation to eliminate the estate tax. Some people are opposed to this legislation. I am going to read you some reasons these people give to oppose this legislation. Please rate each reason on a scale of 0 to 10 with 10 meaning it is an extremely convincing reason to oppose this legislation, 0 meaning it is a totally unconvincing reason to oppose this legislation, and 5 meaning it is neither convincing nor unconvincing. We should cut taxes for the middle class by abolishing the marriage penalty and making college tuition and job training costs tax deductible, rather than giving more tax breaks to multi-millionaires.[6]
Mean = 7.3

0–4 Unconvincing	15%
5 Neither convincing nor unconvincing	12%
6	5%
7	8%
8	13%
9	7%
10 Extremely convincing	38%

Continued on the next page

Sources:
5 *Survey by NBC News, Wall Street Journal, conducted by Hart and Teeter Research Companies, June 19–June 23, 1997.* Retrieved March 15, 2005 from the iPOLL Databank, The Roper Center for Public Opinion Research, University of Connecticut.
6 *Survey conducted by Greenberg Quinlan Rosner Research, May 6–May 9, 2002.* Retrieved March 15, 2005 from the iPOLL Databank, The Roper Center for Public Opinion Research, University of Connecticut.

big difference. Arguments that rely on class inequality or on the undeserved riches of heirs don't have much saliency. Because Americans believe that the wealthy have a right to do as they wish with their money, there is no public up-

Table 4.4. Continued

Thinking about the federal inheritance tax, do you consider this tax too high, about right, too low, or don't you know enough to say?[7]

Too high	41%
About right	5%
Too low	1%
Don't know enough to say	53%

Would you be more or less likely to support a candidate for Congress who voted to eliminate the estate tax, or would it make no difference in how you vote?[8]

Much more likely	13%
Somewhat more likely	15%
No difference (vol.)	46%
Somewhat less likely	10%
Much less likely	9%

Do you think that income earned from wages and salaries should be taxed at a lower rate, the same rate or a higher rate than income earned from dividends, interest, and capital gains and inheritance?[9]

A lower rate	53%
The same rate	29%
A higher rate	9%

Sources:
7 *Survey by Cable News Network, USA Today, conducted by Gallup Organization, January 13–January 16, 2000.* Retrieved March 15, 2005 from the iPOLL Databank, The Roper Center for Public Opinion Research, University of Connecticut.
8 *Survey conducted by Greenberg Quinlan Rosner Research, May 6–May 9, 2002.* Retrieved March 15, 2005 from the iPOLL Databank, The Roper Center for Public Opinion Research, University of Connecticut.
9 *Survey by Public Interests Project, conducted by Greenberg Quinlan Rosner Research, June 17–June 22, 2003.* Retrieved March 15, 2005 from the iPOLL Databank, The Roper Center for Public Opinion Research, University of Connecticut.

roar when television exposés present footage of young heirs and heiresses acting foolishly on their father's yacht or at an exclusive nightclub. Even though most Americans must work in order to pay their bills and survive, there is no strong sense of injustice because the rich "have a right to do so." Previous chapters have even shown that Americans believe that the rich have a right to purchase better educations for their own children. Therefore, framing inheritance in terms of individual rights causes the public to support the claims made by the wealthy and to not perceive the injustice of limited social opportunities for themselves.

Those who favor the estate tax must find a different way of framing the issue. The public should be reminded that ultimately the only people personally affected by the estate tax are the children of dead millionaires. But, by itself, this will not convince a majority to favor the estate tax. Because a majority of the public tends to favor the tax when they are told that it is used for desired programs, one method could be to highlight the usefulness of the tax in terms of education and other important programs. Additionally, from the time of the Boston Tea Party, Americans have despised all taxes, but they especially despised the ones that personally affect them. Therefore, the public might be willing to favor an increase in the estate tax if it were coupled with a decrease in the income tax. Public opinion favors lower taxes on earned income more than unearned income, consistent with the meritocratic ethos.

We might also want to think about shifting from an estate tax to an inheritance tax. If the dead have a right to dispose of their property as they see fit, then changing the subject of the tax might prove effective. Instead of taxing the property of a recently deceased person, the tax could be imposed on the living heir. This could be done with stronger limits on *inter vivos* gifts, higher taxes on acquired property, and even limits on the amount that a person could be allowed to receive as a bequest. It is much more difficult for an heir to say they deserve someone else's property than it is for someone to say they have a right to give it away, especially if it is clear they have not worked for it themselves.

Even though much of the wealth held in America is not a result of earned income but comes instead from inherited wealth transfers, we are not likely to see a widespread movement against those who have inherited economic power. A higher tax on the 2% of decedents who are affected by an estate tax can be viewed as acceptable, if the vast majority gains lower taxes for themselves and more spending on programs they deem valuable. Perhaps in this way America could move one step closer the meritocratic and Jeffersonian ideal.

Notes

1. Jefferson 1944, 488

2. Asked of those employed full time. *Survey by Lincoln Financial Group, conducted by Roper Starch Worldwide, January 14–January 19, 1999.* Retrieved March 15, 2005 from the iPOLL Databank, The Roper Center for Public Opinion Research, University of Connecticut.

3. National adult sample. *Survey by NBC News, Wall Street Journal, conducted by Hart and Teeter Research Companies, December 4–December 8, 1997.* Retrieved March 15, 2005 from the iPOLL Databank, The Roper Center for Public Opinion Research, University of Connecticut.

4. Asked of those employed full time. Survey by Lincoln Financial Group. Methodology: Conducted by Roper Starch Worldwide, January 14–January 19, 1999.

5. Asked of likely voters. *Survey conducted by Greenberg Quinlan Rosner Research, May 6–May 9, 2002.* Retrieved March 15, 2005 from the iPOLL Databank, The Roper Center for Public Opinion Research, University of Connecticut.

6. *Survey by NBC News, Wall Street Journal, conducted by Hart and Teeter Research Companies, April 29–May 1, 2000.* Retrieved March 15, 2005 from the iPOLL Databank, The Roper Center for Public Opinion Research, University of Connecticut.

7. *Survey by Public Interest Project, conducted by Greenberg Quinlan Rosner Research, October 21–October 26, 2003.* Retrieved March 15, 2005 from the iPOLL Databank, The Roper Center for Public Opinion Research, University of Connecticut.

8. *Survey by Lincoln Financial Group, conducted by Roper Starch Worldwide, January 14–January 19, 1999.* Retrieved March 15, 2005 from the iPOLL Databank, The Roper Center for Public Opinion Research, University of Connecticut.

9. *Survey by Money Magazine, conducted by Willard & Shullman, October 21–November 29, 1993.* Retrieved March 15, 2005 from the iPOLL Databank, The Roper Center for Public Opinion Research, University of Connecticut.

10. Asked of American investors. *Survey by UBS, conducted by Gallup Organization, May 27–June 16, 1998.* An older survey with a national adult sample found similar results. *Survey by USA Today, conducted by Gordon S. Black Corporation, April 24–April 29, 1987.* Retrieved March 15, 2005 from the iPOLL Databank, The Roper Center for Public Opinion Research, University of Connecticut.

11. Asked of American investors. *Survey by UBS, conducted by Gallup Organization, May 27–June 16, 1998.* Retrieved March 15, 2005 from the iPOLL Databank, The Roper Center for Public Opinion Research, University of Connecticut.

Chapter 5

Meritocracy Revealed: The Case of Affirmative Action

The contractor will take affirmative action to ensure that applicants are employed, and that employees are treated without regard to their race, creed, color, or national origin.[1]

Lyndon B. Johnson

Affirmative action is among the most contentious public policies in America. Hundreds of thousands of protesters have taken to the streets and those who have a stake in the policy have filed many lawsuits since the policy's inception. The reason affirmative action evokes such strong emotions is that its proponents and opponents make claims that lie at the very core of the American dream. Both sides argue that we should use merit as the distributive rule when choosing among applicants for schools, jobs, and promotions. Both sides are also willing to ignore meritocratic claims to support policies that benefit their own racial group.

Just as with other items related to meritocracy, Americans are conspicuously ambivalent. Distribution by merit is antithetical to distribution by a hereditary or ascriptive characteristic. We noticed in the chapter on inheritance that hereditary characteristics are not necessarily considered to be a legitimate limitation on the acquisition of wealth. In that case, inheriting power is sometimes viewed as just for a variety of reasons. When it comes to affirmative action, Americans sometimes accept and sometimes reject meritocratic principles. This is because the arguments for and against affirmative action pit one meritocratic value against another.

Lyndon Johnson was the first person to use the phrase "affirmative action" as part of a federal plan to end discrimination on the basis of race. Executive order 10925, signed by President Kennedy, established the President's Committee on Equal Employment Opportunity (PCEEO), which was to ensure equal opportunities in employment by the government and its contractors. Lyndon Johnson chaired this committee and believed that an active effort would be necessary to overcome the discrimination of the past (Anderson 2004, 60). Later, Johnson would coin the controversial term in executive order 11246 and continue the civil rights legacy of President Kennedy. Since its inception, affirmative action has been viewed by some as the best possible solution for America's racial divide and has been actively resisted by others.

This chapter will examine the history of affirmative action for the purpose of understanding the origins and purposes of the program. America has often deviated from the meritocratic ideal and affirmative action was implemented in an effort to correct the injustice. Conflicts have been taken to the courts and legislatures and demographic changes are likely to make these conflicts more likely in the future. The chapter will then explore some of the major issues of social justice that are often used to justify or vilify affirmative action programs. Both proponents and opponents seek to combat what they perceive as "unfairness." These two sections will place the public opinion survey data in the proper context. Because affirmative action is so contentious, nothing in this chapter would be considered new to those who have studied the issue. Nevertheless, the affirmative action debate highlights an important tension in the concept of meritocracy. Sometimes it becomes necessary to choose between equal opportunity and race neutral selection procedures when the meritocratic ideal requires both simultaneously.

The History of Affirmative Action

America has a long history of discriminating on the basis of race. At the writing of the Constitution, slavery was entrenched and the Bill of Rights did not protect those of African decent. Whites controlled the government, the press, businesses, and all other social organizations that mattered in America. They used that power to actively discriminate against non-whites, including Mexicans, Chinese, Jews, and any non-Anglo. Racial preferences were the norm and those norms favored whites. Non-whites would slowly gain the same rights that whites possessed, but the struggle wasn't easy.

Each time civil rights were extended to new groups, America witnessed a backlash aimed at reversing the new policies. Abolishing the slave trade precipitated the Civil War. After the Civil War when non-whites were given constitutional protections, southern states created their own laws, known as Jim Crow, to maintain the racial hierarchy. Non-governmental organizations, like the Ku Klux Klan, were created to terrorize blacks and prevent them from realizing their newfound freedoms by harassing and sometimes killing them (Fobanjong 2001).

In the 1950s and 1960s violence erupted as whites actively opposed court decisions aimed at integrating the public schools. Clashes between state and federal troops and between protesters and police became a regular occurrence. Whites actively resisted attempts to provide blacks with the same opportunities they had themselves. They defended segregation in political, social, and economic affairs. Whites, especially in the south, fought to keep blacks out of their neighborhoods, out of their schools, and out of their stores. During that era, as in previous times, whites supported the use of race when making distributive decisions. It was the black leaders who were proclaiming that the use of race was unjust, immoral, and a violation their civil rights.

It was in this context that Johnson's affirmative action policy was spawned. Affirmative action would end the use of race when selecting among applicants for federal jobs. Historians argue that, "[A]ll the administration seemed to be advocating was racially neutral hiring to end job discrimination" (Anderson 2004, 61). Preferences for white employees would be eliminated and an equal opportunity would be given to all job seekers. The plan did not call for quotas, or for any set percentage of minority employees. The initial proposal to ease racial tensions was weak and easily circumvented. The PCEEO did not apply to federal grants and in 1963 southern states accepted $37 million of federal moneys to build or refurbish medical facilities that remained segregated by state and local laws (Anderson 2004, 62).

America's largest corporations, many of which had manufacturing facilities in the south, volunteered to sign a "plan for progress" stating they would make an effort to hire and train more minority workers and desegregate their facilities. Although some major corporations complied with their promises in an effort to maintain their lucrative government contracts, many companies ignored their plans for progress and it became increasing evident that voluntary desegregation plans were ineffective (Anderson 2004, 65; Ezorsky 1991, 35).

After the assassination of President Kennedy, the newly inaugurated President Johnson proposed his sweeping Civil Rights Act that would desegregate all public facilities. The plan was not limited to government property but would apply to all private enterprises that served the public (Anderson 2004, 74; Klinker 1999, 273). Unfortunately, the historic act was not as effective as many would have liked. Because employers could still make decisions based on seniority, newly hired African Americans would be the first to be laid off during recessions and the least likely to be promoted when opportunities for advancement became available. In addition, the use of tests to make hiring and promotion decisions seemed to embody the meritocratic ethos, but the lower levels of education typical of minorities often prevented them from attaining the same jobs as better-educated whites (Anderson 2004, 83).

The "irony of affirmative action" was that companies who only hired or promoted the most able applicant would necessarily only select whites because the segregated system of schools gave white students better skills (Ezorsky 1991, 16). If a company was to integrate the workplace, it would have to hire African Americans with lower levels of skill and try to train them for their new jobs (Anderson 2004, 97). As the Johnson administration pushed for the hiring of African Americans, it began to abandon the colorblind criteria of the Civil Rights Act (Anderson 2004, 99). Integration could not be achieved by simply eliminating "white only" criteria.

As tensions flared and racial violence became commonplace, civil rights groups decided to up the ante. The Congress of Racial Equality (CORE) began to demand that employers hire a certain percentage of blacks to make up for past racial discrimination (Meier & Rudwick 1973). This immediately caused a white backlash as conservatives in Congress began to argue that a system of quotas would discriminate against whites and that such interference in private business was unconstitutional. President Kennedy believed that some compensation was due, but, unlike CORE, did not believe that quotas were a good idea (Anderson 2004, 77).

Among the most ardent resisters of integration were America's labor unions. In Philadelphia only about 1% of skilled tradesmen were African American even though they made up 30% of the population in that city. Federal agencies, supported by both Democrats and Republicans, established hiring goals and required a "good faith effort" to end discrimination on the basis of race (Klinker 1999, 294). Because the jobs required little formal education, it seemed like the ideal place for African Americans to gain access to higher paying employment. Of course, the only way to prove that unions were complying with federal regulations was to measure the increase in minority employees. There was no fixed quota, but it was apparent that unions and employers would have to hire and train black workers in order to comply with the law (Anderson 2004, 117).

The backlash against affirmative action was in full swing by 1968. Conflict erupted between white construction crews and black protesters at federal worksites. White trade union members protested and picketed in cities across the US and claimed that quotas and special preferences were unfair (Anderson 2004, 121; Lawrence & Matsuda 1997, 22). Federal agencies declared that hiring goals were not quotas and officials argued that quotas were already in use to keep African Americans out (Anderson 2004, 118–22). It's illustrative that white resistance to quotas and preferences emerged from groups that opposed integration. They would have preferred a 100% white workforce in their profession and they believed it was unfair for them to be forced to hire and train blacks.

Despite labor union resistance, President Nixon and the US Congress would come to adopt the "Philadelphia Plan," requiring US businesses and labor unions to create an affirmative action plan and establish hiring goals to increase the percentage of minorities in the workforce. The plan would lay the foundation for proportional representation in hiring. To comply with affirmative action policies a company or union's labor force would have to be consistent with the ratio of minorities in the locality where they conducted business (Klinker 1999, 294).

The plan was soon challenged in court. It was argued that quotas violated Title VII of the Civil Rights Act, which made race-based preferences illegal. In *US vs. Montgomery Board of Education* the federal courts defined "quota" as a procedure that "restricts or requires participation of a fixed and inflexible number or ratio of minorities" (Anderson 2004, 126). The Philadelphia Plan did not establish a fixed ratio and was found consistent with Title VII. Moreover, even

though companies would be considering race in their decision making, these considerations were consistent with the stated goal of expanding minority employment in occupations where they had been denied equal access. In legal terms, there was a "compelling state interest" in considering race when making employment decisions. Using race was the only way to get resistant organizations to change their discriminatory policies (Anderson 2004, 127).

By 1972, however, Nixon reversed course and began working against the Philadelphia Plan. He began to argue that quotas were unjust and violated the principles of selection by merit. He also began to tout the often-repeated argument that "two wrongs don't make a right." The use of quotas to give preferential treatment to minorities was viewed to be as wrong as the previous policy of giving preferential treatment to whites. Therefore, no one should be given special treatment and selection should be based strictly on the skills one possessed (Anderson 2004, 139; Klinker 1999, 296). This seemingly race neutral policy, as noted earlier, favored whites because of their much higher average levels of education.

Similar problems existed at America's colleges. In the 1950s many colleges had a 100% white male student body. "At professional schools, deans had quotas, usually admitting only about 5 percent females, which resulted in white males becoming 95% of attorneys, physicians, and professors" (Anderson 2004, 66). Affirmative action plans were adopted at universities to increase the number of female and minority professionals and to increase the percentage of women and minority professors. The most direct stimulus for affirmative action plans at universities were the important federal research grants they received. Unless universities could prove they were hiring more women and minorities, they would be ineligible to receive federal monies (Anderson 2004, 143).

Colleges and universities created policies aimed at recruiting more female and minority students in an effort to increase their numbers in the professions. This would, in time, increase the number of available minority lawyers, doctors, and professors. America's colleges and businesses could then choose from a larger pool of applicants in order to comply with federal anti-discrimination laws (Anderson 2004, 150). It was clear that the universities would have to take action in order to give members of under-represented groups the qualifications to acquire the jobs that employers needed them for.

It is a truism that the jobs that one can qualify for and one's type and level of education are intimately linked. Those that claim that affirmative action constitutes reverse discrimination sometimes argue that unqualified women and minorities are being given jobs that more qualified individuals should have received. The necessary qualifications are obtained at universities, thereby putting universities on the frontlines of the affirmative action battle. How do we increase the number of qualified minority job seekers without creating a mechanism wherein they are admitted into college and professional schools where they can receive the training that qualifies them for higher level employment?

This is the conundrum that the admissions process faces in America's colleges and graduate schools. The medical school of the University of California at Davis believed it had answered that question by setting aside 16 of 100 spaces for disadvantaged individuals. It became apparent, however, that people who were admitted through that special program had lower test scores and lower grade point averages than those who were admitted under the regular criteria for the other eighty-four spaces. Allen Bakke was denied admission to the medical school even though he had an above average test score and GPA. Although he could not be admitted among the regular applicants, he outperformed those who were admitted under the special program. The Supreme Court declared in 1978 that these set-aside places and special rules for minority applicants constituted an illegal quota. But the Court also stated that race could be used as a factor when making admission decisions because it argued that having a diverse student body was a permissible goal of universities. It therefore made set-aside programs and quotas illegal, while maintaining that race could be used in the decision-making process (Barnum 1993).

Whites, who twenty years earlier were defending the use of special rules that gave them the advantage over minorities, were now fighting against special rules that favored minority applicants. Observers note that, "The irony here seems to be that the same ideological group that now use the Constitution and the Civil Rights Act to challenge affirmative action is the very ideological group that were bitterly opposed to the passage of the Fourteenth Amendment and the 1960s Civil Rights Act" (Fobanjong 2001,171). For centuries, among the white majority of America, there was no perceived injustice in the use of different rules for different people. With the coming of the Civil Rights Era these special rules had become associated with the most egregious violations of justice that one could imagine. Similarly, those who twenty years earlier were fighting against segregation and special rules for whites were now defending special rules for themselves, arguing it was the only way to increase their numbers in the professions. A cynic would notice that both blacks and whites oppose race-based preferences except when their own group is being preferred. Indeed, "Self-interest would appear to be one of the major predictors of reactions to affirmative action policies"; those who benefit from affirmative action favor it and those who might potentially be hurt by the policy oppose it (Doverspike, Taylor, and Arthur 2000, 119). Both groups seem to ignore or redefine their own principles of justice in pursuit of their self-interest.

Nevertheless, the white backlash began to have an effect on policy. Ronald Reagan became an outspoken critic of quotas and was able make several appointments to the Supreme Court. Then in 1989 the Court issued its *Wards Cove* decision that shifted the burden of proof from the employer to the employee in discrimination cases. From that point, "it would be easier for a white male to sue for reverse discrimination and more difficult for a woman or minority to win a case" (Anderson 2004, 204). The Congress attempted to reverse the decision by passing a new Civil Rights Act in 1990, but the bill was vetoed by the first President Bush. Although the bill's subject had to do with designating who bore the burden of proof in discrimination cases, the administration gained support for its position by railing against quotas (Anderson 2004, 206; Klinker 1999, 305). Even though quotas were never advocated by the government and were only used by some private organizations between 1968 and 1978, at which time they became illegal, the use of the word "quota" could still be used to stop even modest affirmative action proposals.

A second attempt to shift the burden of proof to the employer resulted in the muddled and self-contradictory Civil Rights Act of 1991. The bill was a compromise between supporters and opponents of affirmative action and was signed into law by the president. The bill confused many and "The Bush administration added to the confusion. The president had vetoed the 1990 act claiming that it would establish quotas and encourage hiring based on race but permitted his Department of Education to continue university scholarship programs that were based on race. He declared his opposition to reverse discrimination at the same time his administration supported set-asides" (Anderson 2004, 213). The bill and the President's defense of it highlight the value conflict that many Americans face. We would like to provide minority groups with real plans that will improve their quality of life and counteract the legacy of past discrimination, but at the same time we are reluctant to use any type of racial preference because these types of preferences are associated with an ugly past.

Moderation on the issue is very difficult to maintain. After the passage of the revised bill, Louisiana Republicans endorsed the flagrantly racist David Duke for governor. As he and other right-wing fringe groups began their anti-quota crusade, moderates began to avoid bringing up quotas out of fear of being associated with racist white nationalists. Those who oppose affirmative action plans have a great deal of difficulty escaping from the racist origins of their views. Even sincere opponents of particular affirmative action plans must come to grips with the fact that they are on the same side as white supremacists. Theodore Shaw of the NAACP said, "Try as I might, I have never with certainty been able to separate the intellectual and ideological descendants of white supremacy proponents from the good faith affirmative action opponents" (Cokorinos 2003, x). The cycle of African American civil rights gains followed by white backlash is, "today, still identifiably the same" (Fobanjong 2001, 1). Small, highly energized groups often have more political voice than their numbers would dictate. Neo-Nazis and the Ku Klux Klan still hold the occasional rally in public squares across America, and when they attack affirmative action, they open the closet door to one of America's hidden skeletons. Because these groups are natural supporters of plans to destroy affirmative action they *ipso facto* make reasoned opposition to affirmative action suspect on racist grounds.

The problem is that white supremacists support the same policies as conservative whites and even overlap in many of their reasons for opposing affirmative action plans. Indeed, "Many of the same politicians who resisted integration and filibustered against the Voting Rights Act in the 1960s have eagerly jumped aboard the anti–affirmative action bandwagon of the 1990s, calling for an end to race-conscious remedies while disseminating malignant racially coded messages with a wink and a nod to old-fashioned racists" (Lawrence & Matsuda 1997, 84). Words like "welfare mother" and "unqualified candidate" provoke images of African Americans and play on white fears of losing their place of dominance in society (Lawrence & Matsuda 1997, 84). What is more, surveys have found that those who rank highly on a scale of "classic racism" (i.e., believing that some races are inferior and accepting harsh stereotypes about other races) are also more likely to oppose affirmative action programs directed at the "inferior" races (Doverspike, Taylor, and Arthur 2000,107).

To be sure, most Americans, including most whites, wouldn't support the overtly racist agendas of white supremacists. However, organizations such as the American Civil Rights Institute, the Center for Equal Opportunity, the Center for Individual Rights, the Federalist Society, and many others have become increasingly more powerful as they lobby, sue, and advertise in a concerted effort to overturn civil rights gains. These affirmative action opponents, "have been able to deftly utilize the civil rights vocabulary formulated to oppose discrimination in order to undermine the moral as well as the legal and constitutional underpinnings of institutional remedies" (Cokorinos 2003, 11). While consistently opposing civil rights and affirmative action, their rationale has changed "from the private right to discriminate to an anti-government libertarian veneer of individual rights and white victimization" (Cokorinos 2003, 18). Even though their rationale changed over the decades, their goals have not. These well-organized and wealthy groups have been able to shape the debate over affirmative action and in so doing have harnessed white anger against civil rights.

By the mid-1990s white resentment had hardened. In 1996 54% of Californians supported Proposition 209 ending affirmative action in that state. A majority of African Americans, Hispanics, and Asians opposed Proposition 209, while majorities of white men and women supported it (Anderson 2004, 256). As a result, the number of African American and Hispanic students who were admitted to the University of California schools dropped dramatically (Anderson 2004, 259; Laird 2005, 38). At UC Berkeley, "the number of black students plummeted by more than half. . . . Hispanic enrollment decreased by 43 percent. Of 3,735 freshman, 126 (3 percent) were black, 269 (7 percent) were Chicano or Latino. . . . White enrollment rose by 7 percent" (Cokorinos 2003, 17). At Berkeley's Law School the number of African Americans dropped from twenty in 1996 to just one in 1997 (Fobanjong 2001, xviii). And at the University of California at Irvine Medical School one African American was admitted. When he chose not to enroll the medical school entering class had no African Americans whatsoever (Laird 2005, 110).

Two years later a similar initiative banned affirmative action in Washington State (Anderson 2004, 261; Cokorinos 2003, 18; Laird 2005, 38). The white resistance to affirmative action that was begun by pro-segregation southerners in the 1960s had, by 1997, finally succeeded in curbing the flow of minorities into America's colleges. In the years after the passage of Proposition 209, increasing numbers of African Americans and Hispanics were being kept out of predominantly white colleges in the states where affirmative action was eliminated. This, of course, was the goal of white supremacist segregationists and means that fewer and fewer minorities will be qualified for the better paying jobs that whites have easy access to. But, not all states have eliminated affirmative action and high achieving minorities in those states that have are choosing to attend very prestigious universities elsewhere (Laird 2005, 172). Still, not all of these students can afford to attend college out of state and many attend less prestigious colleges in their home state while the lower achieving students simply join the lower wage labor force.

Those who oppose affirmative action might adamantly deny racist motivations, but, as a socio-political phenomenon, racism can't be so easily dismissed in the attempt to end affirmative action programs:

> The passionate opposition against affirmative action, for example, cannot be simply explained in terms of resentment against departures from the meritocratic system in the award of jobs or of scarce educational opportunities. People lose in the competition for places at universities or for jobs because of nepotism or preferences for veterans, but those clear departures from the ideal of the meritocracy hardly arouse the kind of passion that race—or gender—based preferential treatment does. Thus, in the context of the *Bakke* case, a state medical school's rejection of a more qualified white applicant to make room for a less qualified minority applicant ignited an intense national debate. But that same medical school favored children of friends of high-ranking university officials over more qualified applicants for admission barely provoked any reaction (Rosenfeld 1991, 2).

It would be difficult to explain this cultural peculiarity without invoking racism as a possible cause. The children of alumni and major donors are often given preferences, as are gifted athletes and those who come from distant states. When the wealthy or powerful are given special considerations, only a few "radicals" protest the injustice. But when an African American is given a special consideration, the protestations of unfairness come from mainstream middle-class Americans.

The white backlash once again led to the courts in the University of Michigan cases of 2003. In *Gratz v. Bollinger* and *Grutter v. Bollinger* the Supreme Court answered questions about the affirmative action policies of the University of Michigan college and law school. In the mixed decision the court found that the college system, which awarded points for being of a particular race, was unconstitutional. The law school system, on the other hand, which used a holistic view and considered many factors in the applicants file without having any set number or percentage of minorities it would admit, passed constitutional scrutiny. Race could still be used to help universities create a diverse student body, but a university could not blatantly favor particular racial minorities by giving them points simply for being a member of a favored group.

Although affirmative action was upheld, the program is much weaker that it was in the past and minorities are finding it increasingly more difficult to succeed despite some victories in the 1960s. They find themselves in a vicious cycle. Because of discrimination of the past they lack many of the social and economic resources of their white countrymen. A lack of economic resources means they cannot afford selective private schools, nor are they able to afford housing in higher-income communities where the public schools are funded at much higher levels than in poor communities. As products of under-funded and overcrowded schools, they are less adequately prepared for college and usually don't advance beyond high school, if they finish high school at all. They will therefore never acquire the qualifications that are necessary for them to become higher-income professionals. This means that they will not be able to afford to pay private school tuition for their children or to live in areas with better public schools. In order to qualify for a good-paying job, one must first qualify for admittance to a good college. Since they need qualifications to get qualifications, they are trapped in the lowest tiers of society.

Worst of all, the white backlash is likely to intensify in the coming years. Most states have not planned for the surge in demand for higher education that has been predicted by demographers. The number of high school graduates is increasing dramatically and large proportions of them will be applying to college. At one time Berkeley could admit everyone who met the minimum requirements; today that is not the case (Laird 2005, 53). Even schools that were once considered "safety schools" are becoming increasingly selective as their applications increase (Laird 2005, 209).

In addition, many states and school districts have changed their formula for calculating a student's GPA. Honors or Advanced Placement (AP) courses are worth an additional point, so that a "B" in an Honors or AP course is the same as an "A" in a regular course. This means that students' GPAs are now on a 5-point scale and,

> Because of the honors grade-point policy, most of those students with GPAs of 4.0 and above did not have straight A's, yet a curious thing happens to many students when they hit that 4.0 mark. They—and, more often, their parents—begin to think of themselves as "perfect" and their sense of entitlement expands exponentially (Laird 2005, 172).

Because of the increasing competitiveness of most colleges, the average GPA of entering freshman has gone up. Berkeley had 8,500 spaces available for the incoming class in 1997. It had a total of 27,151 applications, of which 11,924 had

GPAs of greater than 4.0. It became clear that, "Even if the campus had admitted only applicants with 4.0s and up for those 8,500 fall spaces—the campus was still going to deny several thousand applicants fall admission who had GPAs of 4.0 and above" (Laird 2005, 115). The number of applicants soared in 1998 because of outreach programs and the campus was forced to deny admission to 6,979 applicants with 4.0 or greater GPAs, including 754 minority applicants (Laird 2005, 125).

There were "many stunned white and Asian American applicants and parents" who thought that the end of affirmative action would make admission easier (Laird 2005, 125). In a process that started several decades ago, more and more students and parents voiced their anger at affirmative action programs. Anxiety gripped Californians and, "Almost overnight, one saw and heard fear in the faces and voices of students and their parents. Affluent students began saying—and writing in their application essays—that they were afraid that they wouldn't be able to attain the same standard of living that their parents had enjoyed" (Laird 2005, 67–68). In this climate anything that can potentially reduce the competition for scarce places is likely to be supported.

Discrimination, Affirmative Action, and Public Opinion

Public opinion regarding discrimination and affirmative action seems to be relatively malleable. During World War II most whites in America believed that blacks were an inferior race; they supported segregation, and did not believe that blacks should have an equal opportunity to seek certain kinds of jobs. In 1944 the National Opinion Research Center asked Americans "Do you think that Negroes/blacks should have as good a chance as white people to get any kind of job, or do you think white people should have the first chance at any kind of job?" A majority believed that whites should be given preferences over blacks (Fobanjong 2001, 75). By 1963, however, public opinion had shifted dramatically. Images of police dogs, batons, and fire hoses being used to harass civil rights activists were aired on national television as southern whites actively resisted federal laws. The horrors of white brutality caused many whites to change their long-standing beliefs (Anderson 2004, 73).

In 1970 the vast majority of whites believed that African Americans were being discriminated against. By 1977, however, their opinion had changed. Only one-third of whites felt that way; most did not believe that discrimination or racism was holding African Americans back (Lawrence & Matsuda 1997, 46). And by the mid-1990s many whites were beginning to feel victimized by affirmative action (Anderson 2004, 229). The view that African Americans were being treated unfairly was a temporary phenomenon among the white population

Table 5.1. How Have Lives Been Affected?

Have any of the following things happened to you as a result of affirmative action programs favoring minorities?

	All Whites	White Men	White Women
Not offered a job that went to a racial minority.[1]	12%	15%	10%
Passed over for a promotion that went to a racial minority.[2]	8%	9%	8%
Not admitted to a school.[3]	2%	4%	1%

Have any of the following things happened to you as a result of affirmative action programs that favor women?

	All Men	White Men	Black Men
Not offered a job that went to a woman.[4]	8%	7%	10%
Passed over for a promotion that went to a woman.[5]	7%	6%	11%
Not admitted to a school.[6]	2%	2%	6%

Continued on the next page

Source:
1–6 *Survey by USA Today/CNN/Gallup, March 17–19.* Stacie, Julie, *"Affirmative Action: The Public Reaction," USA Today.* March 24, 1995, pp. A3. Margin of error for the total sample +/- 3%. Margin of error for whites is +/- 4%. Margin of error for blacks is +/- 6%. Margin of error for men is +/- 4%. Margin of error for women is +/- 4%.

It existed in the 1960s and early 1970s and then vanished when brutal beatings of blacks were no longer being aired on national television.

Much depends on how the issue is framed and the extent to which whites believe that African Americans are being oppressed or discriminated against. This framing effect was evident in

> California exit polls in November 1996 [that] had asked voters whether they supported affirmative action programs 'designed to help women and

Table 5.1. Continued

Do you believe that any of the following things have ever happened to you because of racial discrimination?

	All Blacks	Black Men	Black Women
Not offered a job that went to a white.[7]	33%	42%	31%
Passed over for a promotion that went to a white.[8]	31%	42%	28%
Not admitted to a school.[9]	6%	7%	5%

Do you believe that any of the following things have ever happened to you because of discrimination against women?

	All Women	White Women	Black Women
Not offered a job that went to a man.[10]	19%	20%	18%
Passed over for a promotion that went to a man.[11]	13%	13%	13%
Not admitted to a school.[12]	2%	1%	5%

Have you personally ever thought that a woman where you worked got a job or promotion she did not deserve as a result of affirmative action programs?[13]

	All	Men	Women
Yes	19%	20%	19%
No	79%	80%	78%

Continued on the next page

Source:
7–13 *Survey by USA Today/CNN/Gallup, March 17–19.* Stacie, Julie, *"Affirmative Action: The Public Reaction," USA Today.* March 24, 1995, pp. A3. Margin of error for the total sample +/- 3%. Margin of error for whites is +/- 4%. Margin of error for blacks is +/- 6%. Margin of error for men is +/- 4%. Margin of error for women is +/- 4%.

Table 5.1. Continued

Have you personally ever thought that a racial minority where you worked got an undeserved job or promotion as a result of affirmative action programs?[14]

	All	Whites	African Americans
Yes	30%	32%	15%
No	69%	66%	85%

Have you personally ever thought that a well-qualified person at your workplace was hired or promoted as a direct result of affirmative action, and probably would not have been hired without affirmative action?[15]

	All	Whites	African Americans
Yes	24%	23%	32%
No	75%	76%	67%

Have you ever thought that because of discrimination, someone at your workplace received a job or promotion rather than a woman or minority who was better qualified?[16]

	All	Whites	African Americans
Yes	21%	20%	36%
No	78%	79%	64%

Have you ever thought your colleagues at work or school privately questioned your abilities or qualifications because of affirmative action?[17]

	White Women	Black Women	Black Men
Yes	8%	19%	28%
No	90%	79%	71%

Source:
14–17 *Survey by USA Today/CNN/Gallup, March 17–19.* Stacie, Julie, *"Affirmative Action: The Public Reaction,"* *USA Today*. March 24, 1995, pp. A3. Margin of error for the total sample +/- 3%. Margin of error for whites is +/- 4%. Margin of error for blacks is +/- 6%. Margin of error for men is +/- 4%. Margin of error for women is +/- 4%.

minorities get better jobs and education.' Surprisingly, 54 percent said yes, 46 said no—almost the exact opposite of the vote for Proposition 209. In general, citizens overwhelmingly supported civil rights, a majority supported affirmative action if it was defined as giving qualified women and minorities a hand up, but they opposed preferences and greatly opposed anything called a quota (Anderson 2004, 260).

Table 5.2. Providing an Equal Opportunity

Our society should do what is necessary to make sure that everyone has an equal opportunity to succeed.[1]

Completely agree	53%
Mostly agree	38%
Mostly disagree	6%
Completely disagree	2%
Don't know	1%

Some preference should be given in college admissions to minority candidates in order to ensure equal opportunity for a higher education in the U.S.[2]

Strongly agree	13%
Agree	40%
Disagree	34%
Strongly disagree	11%
Don't know	2%

Congress may end up making changes to Head Start in 2003. One proposal is to reduce the federal role in Head Start by giving states control has been described as "damaging" or "dismantling" the program for low-income, at-risk children. Would you be more or less likely to oppose a politician who was accused of voting in a way that would damage or dismantle the Head Start program?[3]

Definitely support	3%
Might support	8%
Might oppose	32%
Definitely oppose	52%
Don't know	5%

Continued on the next page

Sources:
1 *Survey by Pew Research Center, Conducted by Princeton Survey Research Associates, July 14–August 5, 2003.* Retrieved March 15, 2005 from the iPOLL Databank, The Roper Center for Public Opinion Research, University of Connecticut.
2 *Survey by the Chronicle of Higher Education, Survey of Public Opinion on Higher Education conducted February 25 to March 21, 2004.* Retrieved June 26, 2006 from Academic Search Premier.
3 *Survey by Pax World Funds, National Head Start Association, Conducted by Opinion Research Corporation, August 7–August 10, 2003.* Retrieved March 15, 2005 from the iPOLL Databank, The Roper Center for Public Opinion Research, University of Connecticut.

Table 5.2. Continued

Do you favor or oppose the following?

Companies making special efforts to find qualified minorities and women and then encouraging them to apply for jobs.[4]

	All	Whites	African Americans
Favors	73%	71%	87%
Opposes	24%	12%	12%

Providing job training programs for minorities and women to make them better qualified for jobs.[5]

	All	Whites	African Americans
Favors	82%	80%	94%
Opposes	17%	18%	6%

Providing special education classes for minorities and women to make them better qualified for college.[6]

	All	Whites	African Americans
Favors	75%	73%	90%
Opposes	22%	24%	9%

Continued on the next page

Sources:
4–6 *Survey by USA Today/CNN/Gallup, March 17–19.* Stacie, Julie, *"Affirmative Action: The Public Reaction," USA Today*. March 24, 1995, pp. A3. Margin of error for the total sample +/- 3%. Margin of error for whites is +/- 4%. Margin of error for blacks is +/- 6%. Margin of error for men is +/- 4%. Margin of error for women is +/- 4%.

Because Proposition 209 was worded as banning "preferential treatment" it was able to gain majority support.

Most Americans believe that they live in a meritocracy and this view affects their position on affirmative action. Most whites do not believe that they have been discriminated against because of affirmative action. And men do not believe that they have suffered any discrimination as a result of affirmative action programs that favor women. As stated in earlier chapters most African Americans do not believe they have been personally discriminated against, but the proportion of African Americans that do believe so is much higher than the proportion of whites that believe the same. Only a minority of women believe that they have not been offered a job, have been passed up for a promotion, or have

Table 5.2. Continued

Do you believe this is an important role for a college to perform?

Teach students to get along with people from different backgrounds.[7]

Strongly agree	55%
Agree	24%
Disagree	16%
Strongly disagree	5%
Don't know	1%

Prepare students from minority groups to become successful.[8]

Strongly agree	47%
Agree	29%
Disagree	17%
Strongly disagree	7%
Don't know	1%

Do you generally favor or oppose affirmative action programs for women and minorities?[9]

	All	Whites	African Americans
Favors	55%	53%	72%
Opposes	34%	36%	21%

Sources:
7 *Survey by the Chronicle of Higher Education, Survey of Public Opinion on Higher Education conducted February 25 to March 21, 2004.* Retrieved June 26, 2006 from Academic Search Premier.
8 *Survey by the Chronicle of Higher Education, Survey of Public Opinion on Higher Education conducted February 25 to March 21, 2004.* Retrieved June 26, 2006 from Academic Search Premier.
9 *Survey by USA Today/CNN/Gallup, March 17–19.* Stacie, Julie, *"Affirmative Action: The Public Reaction," USA Today*. March 24, 1995, pp. A3. Margin of error for the total sample +/- 3%. Margin of error for whites is +/- 4%. Margin of error for blacks is +/- 6%. Margin of error for men is +/- 4%. Margin of error for women is +/- 4%.

not been admitted to a school because of discrimination. What is more, the vast majority of Americans report that they have never encountered a woman or African American who got a job or a promotion that they did not deserve, nor have they witnessed any discrimination against women and minorities. Fully three-quarters of Americans do not believe that a well-qualified minority has been hired or promoted at their workplace that would not have been without af-

Table 5.3. Opposition to Quotas and Preferences

Establishing quotas that require businesses to hire a certain number of minorities and women.[1]

	All	Whites	African Americans
Favors	35%	30%	66%
Opposes	63%	68%	31%

Establishing quotas requiring schools to admit a certain number of minorities and women students.[2]

	All	Whites	African Americans
Favors	39%	35%	70%
Opposes	57%	61%	27%

Making a certain number of scholarships at public colleges and universities available only to minorities and women.[3]

	All	Whites	African Americans
Favors	31%	27%	51%
Opposes	67%	71%	45%

Continued on the next page

Sources:
1–3 *Survey by USA Today/CNN/Gallup, March 17–19.* Stacie, Julie, *"Affirmative Action: The Public Reaction," USA Today.* March 24, 1995, pp. A3. Margin of error for the total sample +/- 3%. Margin of error for whites is +/- 4%. Margin of error for blacks is +/- 6%. Margin of error for men is +/- 4%. Margin of error for women is +/- 4%.

firmative action. As for the argument that affirmative action stigmatizes minorities, women and African Americans do not believe that their abilities have been privately questioned by their colleagues at school or work. Even when specifically asked about affirmative action, most Americans do not believe that they have suffered from discrimination, nor do they personally know of someone who has. Overall, most Americans don't believe that racial or sexual discrimination is prevalent in our society.

A meritocracy is a society where everyone receives an equal opportunity to succeed, and most Americans strongly believe that opportunities should be made

Table 5.3. Continued

In order to give minorities more opportunity, do you believe race or ethnicity should be a factor when deciding who is hired, promoted, or admitted to college, or that hiring, promotions, and college admissions should be based strictly on merit and qualifications other than race or ethnicity?[4]

Race or ethnicity should be a factor	5%
Should be based strictly on merit and qualifications	92%
Don't know	3%

Would you still feel that way (hiring, promotion, and college admissions should be based strictly on merit and qualifications other than race or ethnicity) if it meant minorities were underrepresented in some types of jobs, or that few or no minorities were hired by some companies or admitted to certain colleges?[5]
Note: Asked of those who said should be based solely on merit and qualifications

Yes	69%
No	27%
Don't know/No opinion	4%

Continued on the next page

Sources:
4 *Survey by Washington Post, Henry J. Kaiser Family Foundation, Harvard University, Conducted by Washington Post, March 8–April 22, 2001.* Retrieved March 15, 2005 from the iPOLL Databank, The Roper Center for Public Opinion Research, University of Connecticut.
5 *Survey by Harvard University, Henry J. Kaiser Family Foundation, Conducted by Washington Post, July 20–September 28, 1995.* Retrieved March 15, 2005 from the iPOLL Databank, The Roper Center for Public Opinion Research, University of Connecticut.

available so that individuals will have a chance to become successful. In line with meritocratic values, a majority believes that our society should do whatever is necessary to make sure everyone has an equal opportunity to succeed.[2] In this vein, most Americans favor policies that "give people a chance to succeed." A small majority believes that some preference should be given to minority applicants in college admissions. A 52% majority of Americans say they would definitely vote against a candidate who damaged or dismantled the Head Start program, which provides resources for early education to children of low-income families. Overwhelming majorities of Americans favor recruitment efforts aim-

Table 5.3. Continued

Which comes closer to your view about evaluating students for admission into a college or university—applicants should be admitted solely on the basis of merit, even if that results in few minority students being admitted or an applicant's racial and ethnic background should be considered to help promote diversity on college campuses, even if that means admitting some minority students who otherwise would not be admitted?[6]

Solely on merit	69%
Racial/Ethnic background considered	27%
No opinion	4%

Applicants to a college whose close relatives attended the same college should be given extra consideration for admission.[7]

Strongly agree	4%
Agree	19%
Disagree	56%
Strongly disagree	19%
Don't know	2%

Continued on the next page

*$p < .05$ ** $p < .01$
Sources:
6 *Survey Conducted by Gallup Organization, June 12–June 18, 2003*. Retrieved March 15, 2005 from the iPOLL Databank, The Roper Center for Public Opinion Research, University of Connecticut.
7 *Survey by the Chronicle of Higher Education, Survey of Public Opinion on Higher Education conducted February 25 to March 21, 2004*. Retrieved June 26, 2006 from Academic Search Premier.

ed at minority applicants that encourage them to apply for specific jobs. Large majorities also support job training and special education classes to better prepare minorities for college. In addition, most Americans believe that it is important for colleges to teach students to get along with people from different backgrounds and to prepare minority students to become successful. Overall, most Americans claim to support affirmative action programs. All of these items would lead one to conclude that Americans would support a variety of programs and policies aimed at increasing opportunities for disadvantaged individuals.

Still, the very same values of meritocratic justice that lead one to support programs aimed at assisting minorities are sometimes used to oppose them. Except among African Americans, there is strong opposition to quotas that force

Table 5.3. Continued

Some people say that because of past discrimination blacks should be given preference in hiring and promotion. Others say that such preference in hiring and promotion of blacks is wrong because it gives blacks advantages they haven't earned. What about your opinion—are you for or against preferential hiring and promotion of blacks?[8]

For	14%
Against	82%
Don't know/refused	4%

Some people say that because of past discrimination, blacks should be given preference in hiring and promotion. Others say that such preference in hiring and promotion of blacks is wrong because it discriminates against whites. What about your opinion—are you for or against preferential hiring and promotion of blacks?[9]

Strongly favors	9%
Favors	6%
Opposes	28%
Strongly opposes	54%

	Whites	African Americans	χ^2	Cramer's V
			183.3**	.263**
Strongly favors	4%	35%		
Favors	6%	10%		
Opposes	28%	28%		
Strongly opposes	62%	28%		

Continued on the next page

*p < .05 ** p < .01

Source:

8 *Survey Conducted by Center for Political Studies, University of Michigan, November 9–January 9, 1995*. Retrieved March 15, 2005 from the iPOLL Databank, The Roper Center for Public Opinion Research, University of Connecticut.

9 *Survey Conducted by National Opinion Research Center, University of Chicago, February 6–June 26, 2002*. Retrieved March 15, 2005 from the iPOLL Databank, The Roper Center for Public Opinion Research, University of Connecticut. Calculations based on the author's own analysis.

Table 5.3. Continued

Do you favor or oppose the following?

Favoring a minority who is less qualified than a white applicant when filling a job in a business that has few minority workers.[10]

	All	Whites	African Americans
Favors	13%	11%	22%
Opposes	84%	86%	68%

Favoring a well-qualified minority applicant over an equally qualified white applicant when filling a job in a business that has few minority workers.[11]

	All	Whites	African Americans
Favors	48%	47%	51%
Opposes	44%	45%	42%

Require private businesses to set up specific goals and timetables for hiring women and minorities if there were not government programs that included hiring quotas.[12]

	All	Whites	African Americans
Favors	50%	46%	71%
Opposes	46%	50%	21%

Continued on the next page

Sources:
10 *Survey by USA Today/CNN/Gallup, March 17–19.* Stacie, Julie, *"Affirmative Action: The Public Reaction," USA Today*. March 24, 1995, pp. A3. Margin of error for the total sample +/- 3%. Margin of error for whites is +/- 4%. Margin of error for blacks is +/- 6%. Margin of error for men is +/- 4%. Margin of error for women is +/- 4%.
11–12 *Survey by USA Today/CNN/Gallup, March 17–19.* Stacie, Julie, *"Affirmative Action: The Public Reaction," USA Today*. March 24, 1995, pp. A3. Margin of error for the total sample +/- 3%. Margin of error for whites is +/- 4%. Margin of error for blacks is +/- 6%. Margin of error for men is +/- 4%. Margin of error for women is +/- 4%.

companies to hire or colleges to admit a certain number of minority applicants. The vast majority of Americans believe that race or ethnicity should not be a factor when making decisions about hiring, promoting, or college admissions;

Table 5.3. Continued

Do you think we need to increase, keep the same or decrease affirmative action programs in this country?[13]

	All	Whites	African Americans
Increase	31%	26%	65%
Keep the Same	26%	26%	26%
Decrease	37%	41%	6%

How likely do you think that each of the following will happen if affirmative action is eliminated. . . . Hiring decisions will be based on merit only.[14]

Very likely	34%
Somewhat likely	25%
Not very likely	22%
Not likely at all	12%
Not sure	7%

Is affirmative action needed? Do you think schools and businesses would or would not provide blacks and other racial minorities with equal opportunities if the government dropped all affirmative action programs.[15]

	All	Whites	African Americans
Would	46%	48%	27%
Would Not	45%	43%	67%

Sources:
13 *Survey by USA Today/CNN/Gallup, March 17–19.* Stacie, Julie, *"Affirmative Action: The Public Reaction," USA Today*. March 24, 1995, pp. A3. Margin of error for the total sample +/- 3%. Margin of error for whites is +/- 4%. Margin of error for blacks is +/- 6%. Margin of error for men is +/- 4%. Margin of error for women is +/- 4%.
14 *Survey by Feminist Majority Foundation, Conducted by Peter Y. Harris Research Group, March 16–April 3, 1995.* Retrieved March 15, 2005 from the iPOLL Databank, The Roper Center for Public Opinion Research, University of Connecticut.
15 *Survey by USA Today/CNN/Gallup, March 17–19.* Stacie, Julie, *"Affirmative Action: The Public Reaction," USA Today*. March 24, 1995, pp. A3. Margin of error for the total sample +/- 3%. Margin of error for whites is +/- 4%. Margin of error for blacks is +/- 6%. Margin of error for men is +/- 4%. Margin of error for women is +/- 4%.

instead they believe that such decisions should be based strictly on merit. Of those that believe that hiring, promoting, and college admissions should be based strictly on merit, nearly 70% would still hold that view even if it meant that few or no minorities would be hired or admitted to college, suggesting there is a ruthless adherence the meritocratic ethos. By the same proportion, Americans reject the argument that race should be a factor in college admissions to promote diversity and they favor decisions based strictly on merit. Many proponents of affirmative action might be surprised to learn that this adherence to the merit criterion includes legacies. A majority of Americans oppose admissions preferences for the children of alumni. While there are no noteworthy lawsuits and not much media coverage on the issue of legacy admissions, most Americans are troubled by the practice.

An overwhelming majority believes that African Americans should not be given preferences in hiring because they believe it would give them advantages they haven't earned. A majority of both blacks and whites oppose the preferential hiring of African Americans because they believe it discriminates against whites. However, there is a disparity; over one-third of African Americans strongly support racial preferences, compared to 4% of whites. A majority of both whites and African Americans oppose the hiring of a less qualified minority applicant over a more qualified white applicant.

When respondents are asked if a preference should be given to a minority applicant in cases where both the white and minority are equally well qualified, the results vary. White opinion is split while African Americans slightly favor a preference for the minority applicant. A majority of African Americans believe that affirmative action programs need to be increased while a plurality of whites believe that affirmative action programs should be decreased. A plurality of Americans believes that, if affirmative action is eliminated, hiring decisions will be based strictly on merit and it seems that only African Americans are fully convinced that affirmative action is needed. The likely reason that a majority doesn't believe that merit would be the only factor influencing hiring decisions once affirmative action is eliminated is the knowledge that social background and personal connections still matter.

Discussion

The perception that America is a meritocracy is enhanced by most Americans' view that they have not suffered any discrimination as a result of their race or gender. When women and minorities are hired or promoted, most Americans believe that they were qualified for their positions and most have not witnessed discrimination against women and minorities. This suggests that, despite the political rhetoric of undeserving and unqualified minorities taking jobs and places at universities from whites, very few people believe that the undeserving are getting ahead. And although some believe that affirmative action stigmatizes its beneficiaries, the vast majority of women and minorities do not feel that their abilities have been privately questioned by their colleagues. The American worldview is one in which discrimination is not readily perceptible.

There is overt support for affirmative action when it is viewed as a program that provides people with opportunities. Indeed, when the words "to ensure equal opportunity" is stated as the reason for preferences, a majority of Americans are willing to support the use of racial preferences. Americans favor programs that provide job training to minorities or that improve their chances of being successful in college. They believe that colleges should teach students to get along with people from different backgrounds and prepare minority students to become successful. This can only be done if colleges are diverse and most Americans, including most whites, support affirmative action programs.

Adherence to the meritocratic norm is found among both African Americans and whites. When an applicant is poorly qualified, there is solid support among both African Americans and whites that the more qualified applicant be hired or admitted. African Americans, like whites, don't favor hiring or admitting a less-qualified minority applicant if there is a better-qualified white, suggesting that merit is a more important value than racial partiality. They also tend to oppose the preferential hiring of minorities because, like whites, they believe the policy discriminates against whites. But this position does not stop most African Americans from supporting quotas, suggesting that, in their view, quotas do not force companies and universities to accept unqualified applicants. Indeed, the brief history of quotas tells us that they were used to force segregated institutions to end their discriminatory policies. For an average African American, quotas are good because they force racist and segregated institutions to accept qualified minorities. In their view affirmative action combats discrimination and gives minorities real opportunities to succeed.

Although both African Americans and whites believe that the better-qualified applicant should be chosen over the less-qualified applicant, opinions begin to diverge in the event of a tie between two applicants. When white respondents are asked to choose between two equally qualified applicants, where one is white and the other is a minority, they can't decide if there should be a preference. Some think there should be, while others oppose the race-based preference. African Americans slightly favor a race-based preference, but the results are not overwhelmingly strong. Among both groups, when two applicants are equally well qualified, there is much more difficulty in making a decision about who should be chosen.

That evidence suggests that in many ways both African Americans and whites accept meritocratic norms and respond similarly to questions of distributive justice. They even tend to oppose legacy admissions. Yet, chapter 3 highlighted a major difference of opinion between black and white Americans. Whites believed that African Americans had about the same opportunities in life as they had themselves, while African Americans believed they had fewer opportunities than whites. This difference is probably a major reason for the differences in opinion regarding the use of racial preferences in affirmative action. If we all have the same chance to succeed, then affirmative action is helping a group that is perfectly capable of succeeding without any help. If we don't all have the same chance to succeed, and these differences are attributable to racial discrimination, then affirmative action provides the discriminated against group a chance to become successful and to compete on a level playing field.

Both African Americans and whites are hesitant about the use of racial preferences. But while African Americans support quotas, whites strongly reject the practice. African Americans, who are much more likely to believe that they suffer from racial discrimination, tend to believe that affirmative action needs to be expanded. Whites, although they support affirmative action in the context of ensuring equal opportunity, tend to believe that affirmative action programs should be scaled back. The view does not stem from overt racism but from a very real belief among whites that African Americans already have an equal opportunity to succeed.

In this context it is easy for many Americans to blame affirmative action for their personal misfortunes; "Affirmative action becomes an easy scapegoat in a world in which we know but don't admit that privilege molds the distribution of everything from college admissions to ice cream sundaes" (Lawrence & Matsuda 1997, 98). When faced with the reality that much of what society has to offer is distributed only to those who have the right connections and are born into privilege, we form a psychological barrier. Denial is as a strong defense for battered women as it is for racial and class oppression. Admitting that those with power are taking more than their fair share is difficult to accept; "It requires either enraged action or total degradation" (Lawrence & Matsuda 1997, 101). As a result, individuals must either "cling to the myth of merit, or accept that" they "are a perpetual chump" (Lawrence & Matsuda 1997, 101). The danger with admitting that the world is not fair is that we might have to do something about it. And, if you're white or wealthy, it means you might have to give up some of your privilege. For many, this may simply be too much to bear.

It's true that the opinions of whites have tempered dramatically over the years, but they find themselves in a very peculiar circumstance. As a group, they tend to support giving minorities more opportunities, but they reject the use of preferences. One explanation is that whites are fearful of losing their privileged position of dominance. Fifty years ago they supported policies aimed at forcibly keeping African Americans out of their institutions. Today they support policies that would reduce the number of African Americans in predominantly white institutions. White sentiment towards blacks has shifted from "we don't want you here" to "we don't care if you're here." They have moved from overtly racist and hostile attitudes to a kind of depraved indifference. Indeed, the typical white American seems to be saying "If ending affirmative action would result in a decrease in the numbers of African Americans in college, then I would still like to eliminate it." This would certainly improve the position of whites, as it has in California and Washington State, and in their view make the world a fairer place.

Relatedly, most whites are in denial about having a privileged position. They firmly believe that African Americans have the same chance of succeeding as whites. Most believe that there are very few barriers preventing blacks from succeeding. This may be because most whites still do not encounter African Americans in their everyday lives. And the African Americans that they do encounter are usually of a similar socio-economic class. If a white professional meets a black professional in the workplace and this is the only black he ever encounters, then it must seem like racial inequality has been solved. The same would probably be true for poor and working-class whites. Because America is segregated economically, the racial minorities we encounter are most likely to be in similar circumstances to ourselves. This would make it very difficult for individual Americans to "see" things from a sociologist's point of view. For many whites, affirmative action is a discriminatory policy that prevents whites from succeeding of their own accord.

Happily, there has been a decline in the overt racism of the 1940s and 1950s. Many whites even support programs aimed at improving opportunities for minorities. In fact, "The assumption that Americans are no longer racist is central to the argument against race-based affirmative action. Opponents of affirmative action proclaim that we have won the war against bigotry and achieved a society that is essentially free of racial prejudice" (Lawrence & Matsuda 1997, 69). Some have called this the "Big Lie" and, if it is believed, then whites can convince themselves that no remedies are necessary (Lawrence & Matsuda 1997, 70). Additionally, "if we can believe there is no racism, or that there is very little, those Americans who benefit from white privilege can continue to reap the benefits of that privilege while denying any moral responsibility for the suffering of others" (Lawrence & Matsuda 1997, 74). It is easier to pretend that there is no white privilege than to acknowledge it and get rid of it, especially since so much effort has been expended in preserving it.

Ultimately, both African Americans and whites support meritocratic values. The issue is that they emphasize different ones. African Americans tend to support quotas and preferences because they believe that this will provide everyone with an equal opportunity to succeed. They don't like preferences, but believe racial preferences are necessary to make sure equal opportunity is achieved. For them, preferences for minorities level the playing field. Whites oppose preferences and quotas because they believe the practices are unjust, but they also believe that equal opportunity is already a reality. For whites, the playing field is already level and minority preferences tilt the odds against them. Most African Americans believe that preferences are a necessary evil that will help us create a meritocracy. Most whites believe that we already live in a meritocracy and that preferences are just plain evil.

Notes

1. quoted in Anderson 2004, p. 60

2. Multiple surveys confirm this, including: Survey by Pew Research Center, Conducted by Princeton Survey Research Associates, July 14–August 5, 2003; Survey by Pew Research Center, Conducted by Princeton Survey Research Associates, September 28—October 10, 1999; Survey by Pew Research Center, Conducted by Princeton Survey Research Associates, November 14–November 18, 1997; Survey by Pew Research Center, Conducted by Princeton Survey Research Associates, November 5–November 17, 1997; Survey Conducted by Center for Political Studies, University of Michigan, November 9—January 9, 1995. Retrieved March 15, 2005 from the iPOLL Databank, The Roper Center for Public Opinion Research, University of Connecticut.

Chapter 6

The Consequences for American Democracy

The proposition that {the people} are the best keeper of their liberties is not true. They are the worst conceivable, they are no keepers at all. They can neither act, judge, think, or will.[1]

John Adams

Every serious scholar of politics has asked himself, "What is the proper relationship between the government and the governed?" and "To what extent should the masses have an influence on government action?" The answers to these important questions often depend on an antecedent question, "Can we trust the public?" If we can trust the public, we might choose to give the masses a great deal of influence. If we don't trust the public, we might be better off restricting their power over government.

When it comes to meritocracy Americans display ambivalence. They sometimes accept and sometimes reject meritocratic norms. Many political theorists are fond of the "value pluralism" idea first espoused by Isaiah Berlin. There are indeed many good reasons to like value pluralism, but when different competing values can't co-exist, choices must be made about which values are preferred in relation to the others. Sometimes we must choose between liberty and democracy, or between economic rights and equal opportunity for all.

Viewed from the perspective of the meritocratic ideal, American public opinion is nonsensical. If, after considering the drawbacks, we decide that meritocracy is a goal worth achieving, then certain rights and liberties must be curtailed. If we decide that those rights and liberties are too valuable, then we must accept that meritocracy is an ideal that we wish not to attain.

Political Theory and Fear of the Masses

Political theory can be divided into two competing schools of thought. There are those scholars who support democracy and who believe that sovereignty and decision-making belongs in the hands of the people. We call these scholars "democratic theorists." Then there are those scholars who hold the public in low esteem and who believe that giving power to the masses is not only dangerous to minorities, but also dangerous to the masses themselves. They would prefer a system of monarchy, oligarchy, aristocracy, dictatorship, or a republic ruled by "philosopher-kings." We call this group of scholars "elite theorists." Sometimes theorists attempt to combine elements of both, making trade-offs that they believe will lead to the best results. And, although democracy has the advantage in the western world, these other forms of government still exist and they have their proponents in the west. Because these other theories are generally less popular, it makes sense to explore what they entail.

Schumpeter, for example, denies the existence of a "collective will" and of a "people" with legal standing. He draws on mass psychology and believes that the "rabble," which he uses interchangeably with "people" and "masses," have a "reduced sense of reality" and are "primitive," "infantile," and prone to irrational impulses. This crowd psychology is described as having a reduced sense of responsibility along with a "greater sensitiveness to non-logical influences." Schumpeter believes that crowds, whether they are a lynch mob, newspaper readers, or a parliament, are easily thrown into a "state of frenzy" which "spurs the animal spirits." He cites cases where clear majorities of the citizenry of a given community or nation have decided to persecute minority religious groups. When this happens democracy destroys liberty. For Schumpeter, any government that is truly *for* the people cannot be *by* them (Schumpeter 1947).

If Nietzsche believes that democracy will lead to the formation of a group of people analogous to a herd of sheep and Heidegger believes that democracy will lead to the formation of a group of individualistic monsters, then Gaetano Mosca would take it a step further and say that democracy will lead to rule by a group of monster sheep. He believed that democratic ideas rouse the base passions and bestial instincts of the ignorant crowd. He argued against the enlargement of the franchise and warned of the terrible consequences of democratization. He perceived the masses to have a herding and fighting instinct, which dangerously combined with a ferocious lust for blood. Instead, Mosca believed "that only the 'scientific study of social laws' by men of 'merit' and 'technical ability' could ensure truly effective government" (Nye 1977, 16).

Vilfredo Pareto made similar claims using rational modeling techniques. From his social Darwinist perspective, he believed that a regular hierarchy of talent naturally develops in social structures. His "circulation of elites" hypothesis argues that elites are drawn from the masses and replace each other with some regularity. He characterized the masses as misfits who lacked character, energy, and intelligence. In the struggle of survival between the civilized man and the savage, he urged elites to use their own violence against the violence of the crowd (Nye 1977, 20–25).

Reinhold Niebuhr, a Christian theologian, emphasizes the brutal characteristics of all human collectives. He argues that one cannot trust the privileged, the proletariat, nations, experts, in short any *group* of actors, to behave in a moral manner. Groups, he says, have a tendency to behave in selfish and anti-social ways and he suggests that both religion and rationality are limited in their capacity to solve social problems. In his view, nationalism, combined with religious fervor, has caused the most terrible cases of human immorality. And while reason checks these selfish impulses, he states, "Men will never be wholly reasonable, and the proportion of reason to impulse becomes increasingly negative when we proceed from the life of individuals to that of social groups, among whom a common mind and purpose is always more or less inchoate and transitory, and who depend on a common impulse to bind them together" (Niebuhr 1995, 35). He further believes that society should strive for justice even if it uses means that do not receive the approbation of moral persons.

These may seem like extreme examples, but even America's Alexander Hamilton felt this way about "the people." He asked, "Has it not . . . invariably been found that momentary passions, and immediate interests, have a more active and imperious control over human conduct than general or remote consideration of policy, utility, or justice?" and "Are not popular assemblies frequently subject to the impulses of rage, resentment, jealousy, avarice, and of other irregular and violent propensities?" (Hamilton, Madison, and Jay 1961, 56). James Madison, like Jefferson, envisioned an elite ruler class, "The aim of every political constitution is, or ought to be, first to obtain for rulers men who possess most wisdom to discern, and most virtue to pursue, the common interest of society" (Hamilton, Madison, and Jay 1961, 350). The common man was simply not good enough to be in control of government.

Indeed no less of a democratic theorist than Alexis de Tocqueville warned that the masses endanger their own liberty: "their passion for equality is ardent, insatiable, eternal and invincible. They want equality in freedom, and if they cannot have that they still want equality in slavery. They will put up with poverty, servitude, and barbarism, but they will not endure aristocracy" thus de Tocqueville warns us of the "Tyranny of the Majority" (de Tocqueville 1969, 250, 506). The various theorists discussed above opposed populist democracy because they were essentially liberal; they feared that the masses would trample on the rights of individuals.

In one way or another these various views of collectives as "inchoate" are an allusion to Condorcet's Paradox, which is better known today as the problem of transitive voter preferences. Condorcet, a French mathematician during their democratic revolution of the late-eighteenth century, drew on the utilitarian's notion of rational action and noted that groups of individual rational actors do not necessarily behave in a rational manner. This simple table demonstrates his theory:

Policy Option	Voter 1	Voter 2	Voter 3
First Choice	A	B	C
Second Choice	B	C	A
Third Choice	C	A	B

Each of the voters has a definite (non-transitive) preference ordering of various state policies designated by the letters A, B, and C. There is a two-to-one majority that favors policy A over policy B, a two-to-one majority that favors policy B over policy C, and a two-to-one majority that favors policy C over policy A. In this case then we have a group of three perfectly (in the economic sense) rational and reasonable people who, when they form a group, will develop a form of schizophrenia.

Modern theorists have found that as the number of actors, but especially as the number of choices, increases, the likelihood of this phenomenon occurring rises dramatically (Riker 1988, 122). There are of course methods of reaching a collective decision (or determining a group's preference) other than majority rule. However, none of those methods would be able to solve the "voting paradox" without violating one of four democratic principles set forth by Kenneth Arrow (Arrow 1967). Procedurally then, there is no democratic mechanism for the aggregation of preferences that is immune from "perverse outcomes." This may account for the elite theorist's view that groups are non-rational, unintelligent, and profoundly stupid. If we value democracy, how can we overcome these problems?

A Few Solutions to the Problem of Mass Irrationality

Arrow points out that one of the ways around this problem of democracy is to have a dictatorship where the policy preference of a single rational individual is always implemented. Although he is not a supporter of dictatorship, his theoretical claim is that reducing the number of decision makers improves collective rationality. But suppose we believe that the public should have at least some influence over government policy. What other alternatives are there?

One method is to restrict the franchise. Although it may seem outrageous to propose this today, it was a truism among America's founders that suffrage must be limited. Early in our history the franchise was limited by race, sex, and property ownership. Later, the American states would impose literacy exams to restrict voting. J. S. Mill regards "it as wholly inadmissible that any person should participate in the suffrage without being able to read, write, and, I will add, perform the common operations of arithmetic" (Mill 1951, 376). But he adds that these basic requirements should be made available to every person. He also believes that "the assembly which votes the taxes . . . should be elected exclusively by those who pay something towards the taxes imposed" because people are prone to spending other people's money immoderately (Mill 1951, 378). Most importantly, however, Mill supported "plural suffrage." He believed that those who were more intelligent, or had superior educations, should have more votes than those who had less (Mill 1951, 386). The actual number of votes each person got was unimportant; as long those with "mental superiority" received proportionately more. Imagine high school graduates getting one vote, college graduates two votes, those with Master's degrees having three votes, and those with Doctorates four votes. Presumably, those who are better educated are more likely to pursue the common good rather than their own personal interests, but that is a subject that is beyond the scope of this particular project.

Another method, also adopted by America's founders, is to limit the power of government. The Constitution would establish bounds that the government could not exceed. Even if the masses found themselves in a state of frenzy with violent impulses, the government would be incapable of action. Dividing power between three separate branches at the federal level and between the federal and state governments furthered the goal of limiting the power of government. The lack of a unitary government made legislative action slow and cumbersome.

Similarly, public policy could be insulated from the vagaries of the masses through a series of "successive filtrations." The first filter is to opt for representative government instead of direct democracy. According to Madison this would,

> refine and enlarge the public views by passing them through the medium of a chosen body of citizenry, whose wisdom may best discern the true interest of their country and whose patriotism and love of justice will be least likely to sacrifice it to temporary or partial considerations. Under such a regulation it may well happen that the public voice, pronounced by representatives of the people, will be more consonant to the public good than if pronounced by the people themselves, convened for that purpose (Hamilton, Madison, and Jay 1961, 82).

Unfortunately, the House of Representatives was directly elected by the people and could therefore, in one single election, be overtaken by the wild passions of the masses who could reconstitute the entire House with men who would pander to their temporary impulse.

Therefore, the next filter would add a second chamber to the legislative branch. According to the *Federalist Papers*, "The necessity of a senate is not less indicated by the propensity of all single and numerous assemblies to yield to the impulse of sudden and violent passions, and to be seduced by factious leaders into intemperate and pernicious resolutions" (Hamilton, Madison, and Jay 1961, 379). The Senate would not be elected directly by the people. Rather, each state legislature would select the persons they thought would best represent their state in the federal assembly. Thus, senators would be chosen indirectly; citizens would vote for the people who would vote for a senator. In addition, Senate elections would be staggered. Only one-third of the Senate would be up for election in any two-year period. The six-year terms of office with staggered elections meant that it would take four years to gain a majority in the Senate and six years to fully reconstitute it. By that time any sudden passion should have dissipated and the danger averted. Again, government change would be too slow to be affected by any capricious whims of the masses.

The Senate would also be smaller in number than the House of Representatives. Madison, although he did not have the mathematical proof, understood Riker's addition to the Condorcet paradox. Madison knew that

> the more numerous any assembly may be, of whatever characters composed, the greater is known to be the ascendancy of passion over reason. In the next place, the larger the number, the greater will be the proportion of members of limited information and of weak capacities... the more multitudinous a representative assembly may be rendered, the more it will partake of the infirmities incident to collective meetings of the people (Hamilton, Madison, and Jay 1961, 360).

For Madison, less people meant better people and more reasoned decision-making. Indeed, "The main reason, perhaps the only real reason, why second chambers exist in all federal systems is to preserve and protect *unequal* representation" (Dahl 2003, 47).

Each of these methods tends to limit the influence the masses can have on government action. The logic is very simple; if we want the best decisions made for our country, we have to start with the best people. Only some, with superior qualities, should be allowed to vote; or their votes should be weighted to give them more influence. These better people will then vote for high-quality representatives. But even then additional filters must be added and explicit limits set on the actions they can take. In this way America's leaders are supposed to be "the best of the best of the best." For those who fear the public, or for those who believe the masses are ignorant, these types of institutional remedies reduce the harm that "the people" can inflict on themselves or on some minority within them.

Value Pluralism

People have different values and these values are applied selectively to different moral problems. Isaiah Berlin developed this view of the moral world and called it "value pluralism." Theorists note that, "He depicts a world in which fundamental values are plural, conflicting, incommensurable in theory, and uncombinable in practice—a world in which there is no single, univocal *summum bonum* that can be defined philosophically, let alone imposed politically" (Galston 2002, 30). The values that Americans share are incompatible with each other and cannot be imposed simultaneously without severe contradictions.

This poses a very difficult problem for those who believe that the public will should be of determining influence on government action. If the public continually contradicts itself, how can we decide what the government should or should not be doing? There are those who believe that the problem is the methods that are used to collect public opinion; if we could only develop better methods, we could gain a better sense of what the public "really wants." They believe that public opinion polls ask "stupid" and "simplistic" questions. If only we could ask better questions, the contradictions would disappear and the public would have rational preferences.

Unfortunately, no amount of methodological advance is going to eliminate the problem of value pluralism. According to Althaus, "the primary culprit is not any inherent shortcoming in the methods of survey research. Rather, it is the limited degree of knowledge held by ordinary citizens about public affairs and the tendency for some kinds of people to be better informed than others" (Althaus 2003, 10). Most people are simply unaware of their contradictory values and preferences. They don't know enough, or haven't thought about the problems long enough, to understand the consequences of their beliefs.

The selective application of moral principles poses a problem when we fail to understand how several seemingly independent ethical preferences come together to form a moral superstructure. While most people simply make moral claims without realizing they are drawing on different principles, some theorists intentionally use different principles to form judgments about the proper distribution of different social goods. Walzer believes that various types of goods belong to different "spheres" and that different distributive rules apply in the different spheres because of the nature of the good to be distributed. This theory is fraught with errors and contradictions that shed light on some of the more problematic elements of American public opinion. It displays, in a vivid and troublesome fashion, what can happen when we sometimes accept and sometimes ignore meritocratic principles.

Walzer's theory of distributive justice opposes affirmative action for many of the same reasons that some Americans oppose it. According to Walzer, "The difficulty with the remedy proposed is that it would require the denial of equal consideration to white candidates who are neither participants in, nor direct beneficiaries of, racist practices" (Walzer 1983, 152). In common parlance, this is the "My grandfather may have done something wrong but I haven't and therefore I shouldn't be punished" argument. We call this an "individual regarding" system of justice. It is proper to punish the wrongdoer, but improper to punish innocent persons. Simply put, individuals should not be held accountable for the wrongdoings of others.

The problem for Walzer, and for white Americans, is that white candidates *are* the direct beneficiaries of racist practices. In 2002, the median net worth of Hispanic households was $7,932. African American households possessed $5,988. Meanwhile, the median wealth of white households was $88,651 (Kochhar 2004). We cannot deny that in the past persons of color were denied employment opportunities available to whites or were paid a fraction of the salary given to white employees holding the same position. This allowed for an unequal accumulation of economic resources over time. Additionally, the use of legal practices such as restrictive covenants and redlining made it difficult for non-whites to invest their money in profitable ventures. The differences in accumulated wealth today therefore reflect differences in the ability to accumulate wealth in years past. This is a direct result of racist practices.

His theory also holds that "the distribution of the family estate belongs to. . . the sphere of kinship" (Walzer 1983, 126), and "we have every reason to respect those men and women who give their money away to persons they love" (Walzer 1983, 128). This means that the beneficiaries of a racist practice can then give that money to their, almost always, white offspring. Though the offspring did not participate in the racist practice of the past, and may not directly participate in a racist practice today, they certainly do benefit from racist practices of the past through their receipt of much larger estates and through economic advantages while growing up.

If we shouldn't let others be punished for someone else's wrongdoing, how could we justify allowing the same others to benefit from the same wrongdoing? If we believe that a son shouldn't be imprisoned for his father's crimes, how can we also believe that the son should keep the money his father stole? The lack of historical perspective in Walzer's statement is troubling, largely because it is probably very common. The theory opposes the unequal consideration of race, just as a meritocracy would, but ignores the gross disparities that give some individuals far more opportunities than other individuals and therefore, deviates from meritocratic norms.

Walzer's theory, in meritocratic fashion, desires an egalitarian provision of primary and secondary public education (Walzer 1983, 210), but then says "parents can hire private tutors for their children or send them to private schools," once again deviating from the ideal (Walzer 1983, 102). Students at the most prestigious private schools come from America's wealthiest families and they receive, so far as we can tell, comparably better educations. Given Walzer's concern about the dominance of money into spheres in which it does not legitimately belong, this acceptance of the market in the provision of education seems contradictory. The persons who are most able to purchase these extra tutors and private schooling are those who have higher levels of economic resources and these, by Walzer's own theory of justice, can come from a single dominant racial group. Let's not forget that of the 400 wealthiest people in America, 56% are from millionaire families and another 14% are from families in the upper 10% of the income distribution (Domhoff 2002, 57). Wealth, unlike income, is largely inherited, and one racial group has a preponderance of this resource. If important opportunities to acquire skills, like educational opportunities, are distributed by the market and there is a strong commitment to market distribution for that good, then opportunities to acquire skills will be *unequal*. Once we justify market distribution for education, education will not be provided equally. This conflicts with the meritocratic ideal, unless of course we could somehow determine a person's potential before they are born. Since this is beyond our capability it only makes sense that each child should be given as much possibility to acquire important skills than any other child.

Next is Walzer's view about the proper distribution of jobs. He says that, "In our culture, however, careers are supposed to be open to talents; and people chosen for an office will want to be assured that they were chosen because they really do possess, to a greater degree than other candidates, the talents that the search committee thinks necessary to the office" (Walzer 1983, 152). This is certainly true and this idea is consistent with the common sense understanding of merit. But Walzer's theory does not attempt to limit the very practices that make it difficult for disadvantaged racial groups to develop their talents.

Instead, it claims that it is just to inherit economic resources, it is just to use those resources to purchase specialized training, and it is just if society selects the best trained, best qualified individuals when distributing jobs. The society that is in line with Walzer's conception of justice is very far from the ideal type meritocracy discussed in chapter 1. Remember that in a meritocracy one's social outcome is not affected by one's race. Walzer's system simply reinforces our society's existing inequalities by claiming that they are just. He does not do this explicitly; rather, by dividing social goods into different "spheres" and applying different distributive rules to the different spheres he ends up with a system that is unjust from a meritocratic standpoint. Although Walzer and most Americans would agree that racial discrimination is unjust and would support the elimination of racist practices, they may also believe it is fair for individuals to receive benefits from ancestors who they recognize had unjust advantages.

Compartmentalizing different goods into different spheres can result in an unmeritocratic distribution of social goods. When jobs are to be distributed by merit, but wealth is to be inherited and training opportunities are to be distributed by the market, then the meritocratic ideal cannot be reached. A person under this system may be able to say, "we distributed jobs according to merit and this is fair because the person with the most talent and best skills received the office." But the society they live in is not meritocratic as long as a correlation exists between non-merit criteria and one's social outcome. This person could adamantly believe that she lives in a meritocracy, but the statement will not be true so long as inheritances and nepotism remain and as long as the opportunities to acquire the skills to succeed are distributed unequally.

We may come to the conclusion that separately each social good Walzer mentions is distributed "fairly." But when combined into a single system we may conclude that the distribution is "unfair." The problem with plural values is that, no matter which value takes precedence in our system of justice, we will invariably violate another of our important values. The key for Walzer, and for every American, is to begin to think about how our separate decisions come together to form a coherent, or incoherent, whole. Everyone should ask themselves, "When do my values contradict my other values?" Only in this way can public opinion be made more rational; only in this way can logic prevail.

We Can't Have It All

If we would like every child to have the best possible opportunities to achieve their potential, we can't have a society that accepts nepotism. If we believe that every individual should work for what they get, then we cannot allow inheritances. This is a classic collective action problem. Individually, every parent would like to provide the best resources to their children; they want their children to have advantages over other children. If every parent does this and some parents have more resources than others, then some children will have more opportunities to succeed and others will have less. However, there are two questions we have to ask ourselves. Do we like this state of affairs? And, is this best for society?

We might very well decide that the costs are too great and that the family must be preserved. But then we must give up the illusion that we truly desire equal opportunity. If we believe it is just for every parent to provide as much as they can to their children, we must accept that not every child will attain their full potential. Nor can we try to convince ourselves that those who work hard gain the right to spend lavishly on their children. Though the parent may deserve all the rewards he or she receives, the child may not. Just as Thomas Paine argued that virtue is not hereditary, we must learn that merit is not hereditary. Merit is "non-transferable." In a meritocracy is not legitimate to say, "I deserve the reward because someone else worked for it, or I deserve the job because someone else has the skills." The moment we accept the hereditary distribution of a good, we reject its distribution by merit.

When Max Weber likens values to gods, he alludes to very powerful forces that affect our behavior. He believes

> that so long as life remains immanent and is interpreted in its own terms, it knows only of an unceasing struggle of these gods with one another. Or speaking directly, the ultimately possible attitudes toward life are irreconcilable, and hence their struggle can never be brought to a final conclusion. Thus it is necessary to make a decisive choice. . . . "Which of the warring gods should we serve? Or should we serve perhaps an entirely different god, and who is he?" (Gerth and Mills 1946, 152–53).

Most Americans may "worship" opposing "gods"; their behavior and attitudes are dictated by opposing values.

In the final analysis, most Americans may not be aware of their own value conflicts when issues of merit are raised. In particular, their belief in the importance of families and in the fairness or duty to assist one's own child by providing them with resources, including inheritances, may not be viewed as conflicting with their view that every child should have an equal opportunity to succeed. This is not because they have resolved the conflict, but because they are not yet cognizant of the internal contradiction. There are difficult choices that must be made after a full consideration of our duties, of our moral principles, and of the costs and benefits to ourselves and to society. Political leaders and educators can lead the discussion, but each individual must form their own opinion.

Among the issues that must be discussed is the role that government should play. When a government is highly responsive to a group of people who have contradictory preferences, then government policy will be at odds with itself. If a strong majority favors the provision of public goods and a strong majority also favors a severe reduction of taxes, then in a democracy the government will tend to have more expenditures than revenues. It will borrow money to satisfy the majority preferences for military defense, for health and sanitation, for retirement benefits, and for other programs of value. In the long run everyone will pay more for the programs we wanted because we didn't want to pay for them. Because we must add interest to the cost of desired programs, we, as a nation, spend more on the programs than if we had just paid for them outright. It is entirely rational for people to want things and to not want to pay for them, but the results are disastrous when an entire people, through their government, does the same. It goes into debt to pay for government services and under-funds programs thereby causing them to be poorly implemented. We can and do simultaneously complain about excessive costs and under-funding. When we decide to eliminate the estate tax, we are decreasing government revenues and saying, "It doesn't matter if everyone works for their money or not." Americans must make a decision because we can't have it both ways.

An Alternative View of the Masses

The critics of direct democracy may be a bit overzealous in their derision of the people. Yet, the people remain largely ignorant and support contradictory policies. What then should we do? According to Althaus, "an appropriate response to information asymmetries is not to attend to paternalistic measures of what the public might want if it knew better, or to consult only the most knowledgeable citizens, but rather to encourage all citizens to discover and act on their interests" (Althaus 2003, 276). Encouraging Americans to learn more about the issues and to come to terms with potentially contradictory preferences is the best course of action. But what should we do in the meantime and what should we do if the public, despite our best efforts, remains ignorant?

Perhaps we should consider the possibility that groups of people are more akin to children than they are to individual reasonable adults or to violent beasts. Children very often do things that are not good for them simply because they don't know any better. Children often express a desire for candy and loudly complain if they get a stomachache. They have two competing preferences and need help if they are to achieve both. Parents may provide their children with candy, but limit its consumption to avoid the negative consequences of eating it. As a society we often want to get to our travel destinations as quickly as possible, but we don't want to get killed in the process of getting there. Our government has enacted laws setting a speed limit, requiring the use of seatbelts in automobiles, and the use of helmets for motorcycle and bicycle riders. In many cases, people need to be protected from themselves. This would be the case even if the self-harm stems from a democratic process.

William Galston gives a poignant example of this principle.

> Consider the following case. While walking through a forest, you come upon two men, one kneeling in a submissive posture, the other pointing a gun at the kneeling man's head and tightening his finger on the trigger. As you rush forward to prevent the tragedy, the kneeling man cries out, "Leave us alone. I gave him permission to shoot me, and you have no right to interfere." I want to suggest that you do have that right, even if no democratically enacted law endorses it. Indeed, I want to go further: You have the right to interfere, even if a democratic law says that you do not. From a pluralist perspective, there are situations (some paternalist, others not) in which the misguided substance of a democratic decision can trump is legitimating form (Galston 2002, 86).

Of course, this conclusion is subject to debate. But when democracy fails us because of competing and contradictory majorities, it may be the place of our leaders, through our government, to choose what is best.

Whether we agree with this solution or not, we should not be dismissive of public opinion. The results of surveys provide information about the public's attitudes, beliefs, and values. Even if public opinion seems nonsensical or contradictory, we nevertheless gain more information by which to make our judgments. In a democracy the people should have a say in what the government does, but when the people can't make up their minds someone will have to do it for them. For this reason representative democracy is better than direct democracy, even if our representatives are less principled than we would like in an ideal world. The role of the people is to elect the best among them and to remove from office those who hurt the commonwealth. A government that is responsive to its people is a good thing to have, but responsiveness without reason or logic is dangerous. Walter Lippmann was essentially correct: the people have a role to play, but their role must be limited for the good of society.

Note

1. Adams quoted in Morone 1998, 33

Chapter 7

Conclusions

The will of the majority is the will of the majority and not the will of 'the people.'[1]

Joseph A. Schumpeter

Majority opinion, when analyzed from the perspective of meritocracy, is contradictory. The public sometimes accepts and sometimes rejects meritocratic norms. Most of the public also seems to believe that America is a meritocracy, yet there is evidence that suggests that many Americans are skeptical of this view. Relying on majority opinion does not yield stable results. It seems, then, that public opinion cannot be used to form a rational or logical set of policy initiatives. It is simply too incoherent to be used as a guide for government action.

Political and social theorists have been discussing meritocracy during the last several decades. Most of this literature opposes meritocracy. It is believed that meritocracy is unjust because it would (1) distribute social goods by intelligence and one's intelligence is arbitrarily distributed, (2) create a genetically based caste system where the most intelligent people take control of every position of power, and (3) destroy democracy in favor of rule by the meritorious. Each of these criticisms has faced counterclaims by proponents of meritocracy. For many, meritocracy remains an ideal utopian society. In the words of one supporter of meritocracy, "a society that does not have its best men at the head of its leading institutions is a sociological and moral absurdity" (Bell 1972, 67). These issues of power and justice are at the very core of political science and we can expect the debate to continue for decades to come.

But the debate will never be complete with out a discussion of public opinion on the matter. If "the people" are to be sovereign, it is only appropriate the people's will direct government policy. In this regard majority rule is a basic principle of democracy. But what if we find that there are conflicting majorities? What if majorities favor and oppose the same policy? Relying on "core values" to direct policy will be ineffective if one core value is used to favor a policy while a different core value is used to oppose it. In this case a choice must be made about which core value is more important. Unfortunately, one of the defining characteristics of a core value is that it forms a foundation for our civilization's way of life. We can't make liberty, freedom, democracy, equal rights, equal opportunity, or any other core value secondary without compromising our own ideals. We may wish to call this the problem of inexorable hypocrisy.

The project finds that Americans are ambivalent in their views towards meritocracy. Americans are not as meritocratic as other studies have found. They do believe that intelligence and hard work should be rewarded, but they also support inherited wealth, seniority pay, and the distribution of educational opportunities through the market. In short, Americans are not strictly meritocratic in their distributive preferences. They often consider items other than merit to be legitimate reasons for inegalitarian modes of distribution. Having put in place a description of the ideal type meritocratic society, we can see that these latter attitudes and values compromit the meritocratic ones.

The American public does not have the same set of concerns as many social theorists. Unlike Rawls, most Americans believe it is fair for more intelligent people to earn more money. Unlike Herrnstein and Murray, most Americans don't believe that success is genetically determined; it is therefore doubtful that they would be afraid that a genetically based caste system would form. Most Americans do value democracy and wouldn't want experts to make government policy in place of their elected officials. Therefore Dahl's concern may not be a serious threat. Some theorists have tried to blend democratic and meritocratic theory, suggesting that these two visions are complementary rather than antagonistic. While the "highbrow" debate is important, the "lowbrow" understanding of the issues is paramount in any society that is serious about democracy.

One particularly interesting finding of this project calls into question Hochschild's assertion that Americans are egalitarian in the social domain. Although the data presented in this project more or less confirmed that Hochschild was correct about Americans' attitudes in the economic and political domains, it also finds that Americans are not social egalitarians. Most Americans believe it is perfectly just and fair for people to be given greater levels of respect and deference and to have higher social status if their jobs require great amounts of skill or if they make the most of the opportunities they had in life.

Previous studies have also shown that Americans believe that the US is a meritocratic society where intelligence and hard work is actually rewarded. The majority believes that everyone in America has an equal opportunity to succeed, yet a substantial proportion believes that race, gender, social background, and personal connections make a difference in one's outcome in life. The *vox populi* tells us that America is and is not a meritocracy. There are elements of both in America.

The low level of "ideological constraint" found in mass opinion is not new. But it does present a recurring problem in the study of government and politics. Exactly how much power should the people have in a democracy? Some theorists have argued that because of the public's ignorance the power that the masses could yield on government should be limited. This was true even of the American founders. Yet, if we value democracy, the people should have an important influence on government policy. Public opinion should not be ignored, even if the results are nonsensical, irrational, and illogical. The public has a role to play, but the populist dream of a direct democracy cannot long withstand the contradictory preferences held by competing majorities. Decisions must be made, and our elected leaders must make them.

Still, the public should make an effort at understanding its self-contradictory attitudes, values, and beliefs. Individuals are much more capable of rationality than groups, and through education and public discussion individuals can come to grips with the competing values that currently muddle their expressed preferences. Educators can ask students the difficult questions and political leaders can spark a public discussion about the difficult choices that must be made.

Note

1. Schumpeter 1947, 272

Bibliography

ABC News/Louis Harris and Associates Survey. December 21–December 26, 1978. Retrieved March 15, 2005 from the iPOLL Databank, The Roper Center for Public Opinion Research, University of Connecticut.

Abdullah, Saiful Azhar. "Culture of meritocracy a step towards distinction, says Najib." *New Straits Times* (Malaysia) (September 22, 2004), p. 1.

Adonis, Andrew. "Our classless self-delusion (the old hierarchy may have gone but a new one has taken its place)." *New Statesman* 126 (October 3, 1997): 23.

Aggassi, Joseph. "Academic Democracy Threatened—The Case of Boston University." *Interchange* 21, no. 2 (1990): 26–34.

Alexander, Karl, Martha Cook, and Edward L. McDill, "Curriculum Tracking and Educational Stratification: Some Further Evidence," *American Sociological Review* 43 (February 1978): 47–66.

Alger, Horatio Jr. *Making His Way, Or Frank Courtney's Struggle Upward.* New York: Arno Press (1974).

———. *Ragged Dick and Mark, The Match Boy: Two Novels By Horatio Alger.* New York: Macmillan (1962).

Althaus, Scott L. *Collective Preferences in Democratic Politics: Opinion Surveys and the Will of the People.* New York: Cambridge University Press (2003).

Alves, Wayne, and Peter Rossi. "Who Should Get What? Fairness Judgments of the Distribution of Earnings." *American Journal of Sociology* 84, iss. 3 (November 1978): 541–64.

Ambercrombie, Nicholas, Alan Ward, et. al. *Contemporary British Society.* 3rd ed. Malden, MA: Polity Press (2000).

Anderson, Terry H. *The Pursuit of Fairness: A History of Affirmative Action.* New York: Oxford University Press (2004).

Andreoni, James. "Comments on Paul G. Shervish and John J. Havens 'Gifts and Bequests: Family or Philanthropic Organizations.'" In Alicia H. Munnell and Annika Sundén (eds.), *Death and Dollars: The Role of Gifts and Bequests in America.* Washington, D.C.: Brookings Institution Press (2003).

Arrow, Kenneth J. "Public and Private Values." In Sidney Hook (ed.), *Human Values and Economic Policy.* New York: New York University Press (1967).

Barnum, David G. *The Supreme Court & American Democracy.* New York: St. Martin's Press (1993).

Barry, John W. "Meritocracy defended (review article)." *Public Interest*, no. 19 (Spring 1995): 129–33.

Bell, Daniel. *The Coming of Post-Industrial Society: A venture in social forecasting.* New York: Basic Books (1973).

———. "The Information Society." In Michael L. Dertouzos and Joel Moses (eds.), *The Computer Age: a twenty—year view*. Cambridge: MIT Press (1979).

———. "On Meritocracy and Equality." *Public Interest* (November 1972).

Bellow, Adam. *In Praise of Nepotism: A Natural History*. New York: Double Day (2003).

Bentley, Authur F. *The Process of Government: A Study of Social Pressures*. Chicago: The University of Chicago Press (1908).

Berelson, Bernard R., Paul F. Lazarsfeld, and William N. McPhee. *Voting: A Study of Opinion Formation in a Presidential Campaign*. Chicago: The University of Chicago Press (1954).

Bishop, George F., Robert W. Oldendick, and Alfred J. Tuchfarber. "Effects of Question Wording and Format on Political Attitude Consistency." *Public Opinion Quarterly* 42, no. 1 (Spring 1978): 81–92.

Blau, Peter M., and O. D. Duncan. *The American Occupational Structure*. New York: John Wiley & Sons (1967).

Born Rich. Dir. Jamie Johnson. With Georgianna Bloomberg, Stephanie Ercklentz, Cody Franchetti, Christina Floyd, Juliet Hartford, Josiah Hornblower, Jamie Johnson, S. I. Newhouse IV, Ivanka Trump, Luke Weill, and Carlo von Zeitschel. Writ. Jamie Johnson. Shout Factory (2004).

Boudon, Raymond. *The Origin of Values: Sociology and Philosophy of Beliefs*. New Brunswick: Transaction Publishers (2001).

Bowles, Samuel, and Herbert Gintis. *Schooling in Capitalist America: Educational Reform and the Contradictions of Economic Life*. New York: Basic Books (1976).

Bracewell-Milnes, Barry. *Euthanasia for Death Duties: Putting Inheritance Tax Out of Its Misery*. London: Institute of Economic Affairs (2002).

Breen, Richard, and John Goldthorpe. "Class inequality and meritocracy: a critique of Saunders and an alternative analysis." *British Journal of Sociology* 50, no. 1 (March 1999): 1–27.

Brittain, John A. *The Inheritance of Economic Status*. Washington, D.C.: The Brookings Institution (1977).

Broman, S. H., P. L. Nichols and W. A. Kennedy. *Preschool IQ: Prenatal and Early Developmental Correlates*. Hillsdale, NJ: Erlbaum. (1975).

Bruce-Briggs, B., ed. *The New Class?* New Brunswick: Transaction Books (1979).

Cable News Network and USA Today. Survey conducted by Gallup Organization, January 13–January 16, 2000. Retrieved March 15, 2005 from the iPOLL Databank, The Roper Center for Public Opinion Research, University of Connecticut.

Cable News Network and USA Today. Survey conducted by Gallup Organization, June 22–June 25, 2000. Retrieved March 15, 2005 from the iPOLL

Databank, The Roper Center for Public Opinion Research, University of Connecticut.

Campbell, Angus, Philip E. Converse, Warren E. Miller, and Donald E. Stokes. *The American Voter: An Abridgement*. New York: John Wiley & Sons (1964).

Cawley, John, James Heckman, Lance Lochner, and Edward Vytlacil. "Understanding the Role of Cognitive Ability in Accounting for the Recent Rise in the Economic Return to Education." In Kenneth Arrow, Samuel Bowles, and Steven Durlauf. (eds.), *Meritocracy and Economic Inequality*. Princeton: Princeton University Press (2000).

CBS News/New York Times Survey. October 29–November 1, 1994. Retrieved March 15, 2005 from the iPOLL Databank, The Roper Center for Public Opinion Research, University of Connecticut.

Center for Political Studies, University of Michigan Survey. November 9–January 9, 1995. Retrieved March 15, 2005 from the iPOLL Databank, The Roper Center for Public Opinion Research, University of Connecticut.

Chang, Weining C. "Toward equal opportunities: fairness, values, and affirmative action programs in the U. S." *Journal of Social Issues* 52 (Winter 1996): 93–97.

Chester, Ronald. *Inheritance, Wealth, and Society*. Bloomington: Indiana University Press (1982).

Children's Research & Education Institute. Survey conducted by Greenberg Quinlan Rosner Research & Public Opinion Strategies, January 8–January 13, 2003. Retrieved February 22, 2005 from the iPOLL Databank, The Roper Center for Public Opinion Research, University of Connecticut.

Chronicle of Higher Education, Survey of Public Opinion on Higher Education. February 25 to March 21, 2004. Retrieved June 26, 2006 from Academic Search Premier.

Citrin, Jack, Donald Philip Green, and David O. Sears. "White Reactions to Black Candidates: When Does Race Matter?" *Public Opinion Quarterly* 54, no. 1 (Spring 1990): 74–96.

Citrin, Jack, Beth Reingold, and Donald P. Green "American Identity and the Politics of Ethnic Change." *The Journal of Politics* 52, no. 4 (November 1990): 1124–54.

Clark, Terry Nichols. "The Irish Ethic and the Spirit of Patronage." *Ethnicity* 2, (1975): 305–59.

———. "Old and New Paradigms for Urban Research," *Urban Affairs Review* 36, no. 1 (September 2000): 3–45.

Clark, Terry Nichols, and Vincent Hoffmann-Martinot, eds. *The New Political Culture*. Boulder: Westview Press (1998).

Cokorinos, Lee. *An Assault on Diversity: An Organized Challenge to Racial and Gender Justice*. Lanham, MD: Rowman & Littlefield (2003).

Cookson, Peter W., and Caroline Hodges Persell. *Preparing for Power: America's Elite Boarding Schools*. New York: Basic Books (1985).

Converse, Philip E. "The Nature of Belief Systems in Mass Publics." In David Apter (ed.), *Ideology and Discontent*. New York: Free Press (1964).

———. "Attitudes and Non-Attitudes: Continuation of a Dialogue." In Edward R. Tuft. *The Quantitative Analysis of Social Problems*. ed. Boston: Addison-Wesley (1970).

Council for Excellence in Government and Partnership for Public Service. Survey conducted by Hart and Teeter Research Companies, July 31–August 8, 2001. Retrieved March 15, 2005 from the iPOLL Databank, The Roper Center for Public Opinion Research, University of Connecticut.

Dahl, Robert A. *Democracy in the United States: Promises and Performance*, 2nd ed. Chicago: Rand McNally (1967).

———. *Democracy and Its Critics*. New Haven: Yale University Press (1989).

———. *How Democratic Is the American Constitution?* New Haven: Yale University Press (2003).

Darling-Hammond, Linda. *The Right to Learn: A Blueprint for Creating Schools That Work*. San Francisco: Jossey-Bass Publishers (1997).

Dawson, Michael C. *Behind the Mule: Race and Class in African-American Politics*. Princeton: Princeton University Press (1994).

Delong, J. Bradford. "A History of Bequests in the United States." In Alicia H. Munnell and Annika Sundén (eds.), *Death and Dollars: The Role of Gifts and Bequests in America*. Washington, D.C.: Brookings Institution Press (2003).

Democratic Leadership Council. Survey conducted by Penn, Schoen & Berland Associates, July 30–August 2, 1998. Retrieved March 15, 2005 from the iPOLL Databank, The Roper Center for Public Opinion Research, University of Connecticut.

De Nardi, Mariacristina. "Two Essays on Life-Cycle Economics." Diss., University of Chicago (1999).

DeParle, Jason. "Daring Research or 'Social Science Pornography?'" *The New York Times Magazine* (October 09, 1994): 48.

de Tocqueville, Alexis. *Democracy in America*. Translated by George Lawrence, edited by J. P. Mayer. New York: Harper (1969).

Diamond, Peter A. "Comments on J. Bradford Delong 'A History of Bequests in the United States.'" In Alicia H. Munnell and Annika Sundén (eds.), *Death and Dollars: The Role of Gifts and Bequests in America*. Washington, D.C.: Brookings Institution Press (2003).

Dickens, William T. and James R. Flynn "Heritability Estimates Versus Large Environmental Effects: The IQ Paradox Resolved." *Psychological Review* v. 108, iss. 2 (April 1, 2001): 346–69.

Domhoff, G. William. *Who Rules America?* 4th ed. New York: McGraw-Hill (2002).

Doverspike, Dennis, Mary Anne Taylor, and Winfred Arthur, Jr. *Affirmative Action: A Psychological Perspective*. Huntington: Nova Science Publishers (2000).

Drake, W. Avon, and Robert D. Holsworth. *Affirmative Action and the Stalled Quest for Black Progress*. Urbana, IL: University of Illinois Press (1996).

Dreeben, Robert. *On What is Learned in School*. Reading: Addison-Wesley (1968).

Ezorsky, Gertrude. *Racism and Justice: The Case for Affirmative Action*. Ithaca, NY: Cornell University Press (1991).

Feminist Majority Foundation. Survey conducted by Peter Y. Harris Research Group, March 16–April 3, 1995. Retrieved March 15, 2005 from the iPOLL Databank, The Roper Center for Public Opinion Research, University of Connecticut.

Fischer, Claude S., et. al. *Inequality by Design: Cracking the Bell Curve Myth*. Princeton: Princeton University Press (1996).

Flynn, James R. "Searching for justice: the discovery of IQ gains over time." *American Psychologist* 54, no. 1 (January 1999): 5–20.

Fobanjong, John. *Understanding the Backlash Against Affirmative Action*. Huntington: Nova Science Publishers (2001).

Fox News. Survey conducted by Opinion Dynamics, July 12–July 13, 2000. Retrieved March 15, 2005 from the iPOLL Databank, The Roper Center for Public Opinion Research, University of Connecticut.

Fraser, Steven. ed. *The Bell Curve Wars: Race. Intelligence, the Future of America*. New York: Basic Books (1995).

Freedman, Samuel G. "Dreamed You Didn't Study? Be Proud, You Meritocrat." *The New York Times* (September 8, 2004): Section B, p. 8.

Friedman, Milton. *Capitalism and Freedom*. Chicago: University of Chicago Press (1962 [2002]).

Frohlich, Norman, Joe Oppenheimer, and Anja Kurki. "Modeling Other—Regarding Preferences and an Experimental Test." *Public Choice* 119, iss. 1–2 (April 2004): 91–117.

Fullinwider, Robert, and Judith Lichtenberg. *Leveling the Playing Field: justice, politics, and college admissions*. Lanham, MD: Rowman & Littlefield (2004).

Gale, William G., and Samara Potter. "The Impact of Gifts and Bequests on Aggregate Saving and Capital Accumulation." In Alicia H. Munnell and Annika Sundén (eds.), *Death and Dollars: The Role of Gifts and Bequests in America*. Washington, D.C.: Brookings Institution Press (2003).

Gallup Organization Survey. February 19–February 21, 2001. Retrieved March 15, 2005 from the iPOLL Databank, The Roper Center for Public Opinion Research, University of Connecticut.

Gallup Organization Survey. June 12–June 18, 2003. Retrieved March 15, 2005 from the iPOLL Databank, The Roper Center for Public Opinion Research, University of Connecticut.

Gallup Organization Survey. April 5–April 8, 2004. Retrieved March 15, 2005 from the iPOLL Databank, The Roper Center for Public Opinion Research, University of Connecticut.

Galston, William A. *Liberal Pluralism: The Implications of Value Pluralism for Political Theory and Practice*. New York: Cambridge University Press (2002).

Garnier, Maurice, and Jerald Hage. "Class Formation, Politics, and Institutions: Schooling in the United States." *Sociology of Education* 64, no. 4 (October 1991): 229–50.

General Motors Corporation. Survey conducted by Gallup Organization, April 23—May 31, 1998. Retrieved February 22, 2005 from the iPOLL Databank, The Roper Center for Public Opinion Research, University of Connecticut.

Gerth, H. H., and C. Wright Mills. *From Max Weber: Essays in Sociology*. New York: Oxford University Press (1946).

Gilliland, Stephen W. "The Perceived Fairness of Selection: An Organizational Justice Perspective." *The Academy of Management Review* 18, iss. 4 (October 1993): 694–734.

Ginsberg, Benjamin. *The Captive Public: How Mass Opinion Promotes State Power*. New York: Basic (1986).

Glynn, Carroll, et. al. *Public Opinion*. Boulder: Westview Press (1999).

Gouldner, Alvin W. *The Future of Intellectuals and the Rise of the New Class: a frame of reference, theses conjectures, arguments, and an historical perspective on the role of intellectuals and intelligentsia in the international class contest of the modern era*. New York: Continuum Books (1979).

Greenberg Quinlan Rosner Research Survey. May 6–May 9, 2002. Retrieved March 15, 2005 from the iPOLL Databank, The Roper Center for Public Opinion Research, University of Connecticut.

Greenspan, Stephen, and John Driscoll. "The Role of Intelligence in a Broad Model of Personal Competence." In Dawn Flanagan et. al., *Contemporary Intellectual Assessment: Theories, Tests and Issues*. New York: The Guilford Press (1997).

Hamilton, Alexander, James Madison, and John Jay. *The Federalist Papers*. New York: Mentor (1961)

Hari, Johann. "A Defining Cause for the Labour Party." *The Independent* (January 19, 2005): First Edition, p. 33.

Harvard University and Henry J. Kaiser Family Foundation. Survey conducted by Washington Post, July 20–September 28, 1995. Retrieved March 15, 2005 from the iPOLL Databank, The Roper Center for Public Opinion Research, University of Connecticut.

Haslett, D. W. "Distributive Justice and Inheritance." In Guido Erreygers and Toon Vandevelde. (eds.) *Is Inheritance Legitimate?: Ethical and Economic Aspects of Wealth Transfers*. Heidelberg: Springer (1997).

Hattersley, Roy. "Up and down the social latter (meritocracy doesn't work but T. Blair doesn't know why)." *New Statesman* 128, no. 4420 (January 22, 1999): 25–27.

Hayek, Fredrich A. *The Constitution of Liberty*. Chicago: University of Chicago Press (1960).

———. *The Road to Serfdom*. Chicago: University of Chicago Press (1944).

Henry, William A. *In Defense of Elitism*. New York: Anchor Books (1994).

Herrnstein, Richard J. *I.Q. in the Meritocracy*. Boston: Atlantic Monthly Press (1971).

———. "Whatever Happened to Vaudeville? A reply to professor Chomsky." In N. J. Block and Gerald Dworkin (eds.), *The IQ Controversy: Critical Readings*. New York: Pantheon Books (1976).

Hochschild, Jennifer. *What's Fair: American Beliefs about Distributive Justice*. Cambridge: Harvard University Press (1981).

———. *Facing Up to the American Dream: Race, Class, and the Soul of the Nation*. Princeton: Princeton University Press (1995).

Howe, Michael J. A. *IQ in Question: The Truth about Intelligence*. London: Sage Publications (1997).

Hurd, Michael D. "Bequests: By Accident or Design." In Alicia H. Munnell and Annika Sundén (eds.), *Death and Dollars: The Role of Gifts and Bequests in America*. Washington, D.C.: Brookings Institution Press (2003).

Hurley, Patricia A., and Kim Quaile Hill. "The Prospects for Issue-Voting in Contemporary Congressional Elections." *American Politics Quarterly* 8 iss. 4 (October 1980): 425.

Investor's Business Daily and Christian Science Monitor. Survey conducted by TIPP-Techno Metrica Institute of Policy and Politics, February 8–February 12, 2001. Retrieved March 15, 2005 from the iPOLL Databank, The Roper Center for Public Opinion Research, University of Connecticut.

Iyengar, Shanto, and Donald Kinder. *News that Matters: Television and American Opinion*. Chicago: University of Chicago Press (1987).

Jackson-Leslie, Llenda. "Race, sex, and meritocracy." *Black Scholar* 25 (Summer 1995): 24–29.

Jefferson, Thomas. *The Life and Selected Writings of Thomas Jefferson*. Adrienne Koch and William Penn (eds.). New York: The Modern Library (1944).

Jencks, Christopher, and Mary Jo Bane. "Five myths about your IQ" In N. J. Block and Gerald Dworkin. (eds.), *The IQ Controversy: Critical Readings*. New York: Pantheon Books (1976).

Jennings, Kent. "Ideological Thinking Among Mass Publics and Political Elites." *Public Opinion Quarterly* 56 (1992): 419–41.

Johnson, Barry W., and Martha Britton Eller. "Federal Taxation of Inheritance and Wealth Transfers." In Robert K. Miller Jr. and Stephan J. McNamee (eds.), *Inheritance and Wealth in America*. New York: Plenum Press (1998).

Johnson, Lyndon B. *Public Papers of the Presidents of the United States: Lyndon B. Johnson 1965*. Vol. II, entry 301, Washington, D.C.: Government Printing Office (1966).

Kalleberg, Arne L., and Karyn A. Loscocco. "Aging, Values, and Rewards: Explaining Age Differences in Job Satisfaction." *American Sociological Review* 48, no. 1 (February 1983): 78–90.

Kamphaus, R. W., Martha D. Petoskey, and Anna Walters Morgan. "A History of Intelligence Test Interpretation." In Dawn Flanagan, et. al., *Contemporary Intellectual Assessment: Theories, Tests and Issues*. New York: The Guilford Press (1997).

Kaplan, Linda Duhan, and Charles Kaplan. "Democracy, Meritocracy, and the Cognitive Elite: The Real Thesis of the Bell Curve." *Educational Theory* 47, no. 3 (Summer 1997): 425–31.

Kaufmann, Karen M., and John R. Petrocik. "The Changing Politics of American Men: Understanding the Sources of the Gender Gap" *American Journal of Political Science* 43, no. 3 (July 1999): 864–87.

Kerckhoff, Alan C. *Diverging Pathways: Social Structure and Career Deflections*. Cambridge: Cambridge University Press (1993).

Kerckhoff, Alan C., Richard Campbell, and Jerry M. Trott. "Dimensions of Educational and Occupational Attainment in Great Britain." *American Sociological Review* 47 (June 1982): 347–64.

Klinker, Philip A., with Rogers M. Smith. *The Unsteady March: The Rise and Decline of Racial Equality in America*. Chicago: The University of Chicago Press (1999).

Kochhar, Rakesh. *The Wealth of Hispanic Households: 1996 to 2002*. Pew Hispanic Center (2004), accessed December 15, 2004, www.pewhispanic.org/site/docs/pdf/The%20Wealth%20of%20Hispanic%20Households.pdf.

Konow, James. "Fair Shares and Cognitive Dissonance in Allocation Decisions." *American Economic Review* 90, iss. 4 (September 2000): 1072–91.

———. "A Positive Theory of Economic Fairness." *Journal of Economic Behavior and Organization* 31, iss. 1 (October 1996): 15–35.

Kopczuk, Wojciech, and Joel Slemrod. "Tax Consequences on Wealth Accumulation and Transfers of the Rich." In Alicia H. Munnell and Annika Sundén (eds.), *Death and Dollars: The Role of Gifts and Bequests in America*. Washington, D.C.: Brookings Institution Press (2003).

Korenman, Sanders, and Christopher Winship. "A Reanalysis of *The Bell Curve*: Intelligence, Family Background, and Schooling." In Kenneth Arrow, Samuel Bowles, and Steven Durlauf. (eds.), *Meritocracy and Economic Inequality*. Princeton: Princeton University Press (2000).

Kozol, Jonathan. *Savage Inequalities: Children in America's Schools.* New York: Harper (1991).

Kull, Steven. "Expecting More Say: the American public on its role in government decision making." Washington D.C.: Center for Policy Attitudes (May 1999).

Kull, Steven, and I. M. Destler. *Misreading the Public: The Myth of a New Isolationism.* Washington D.C.: Brookings Institution Press (1999).

Laird, Bob. *The Case for Affirmative Action in University Admissions.* Berkeley, CA: Bay Tree Publishing (2005).

Lampard, Richard. "Might Britain be a meritocracy? A comment on Saunders." *Sociology* 30 (May 1996): 387–93.

Lasch, Christopher. *The Revolt of the Elites and The Betrayal of Democracy.* New York: W.W. Norton & Company (1995).

Lasswell, Harold D. *Power and Personality.* New York: W.W. Norton & Company (1976). Originally published by W.W. Norton & Company in 1948.

Lawrence, Charles R. III, and Mari J. Matsuda. *We Won't Go Back: Making the Case for Affirmative Action.* New York: Houghton Mifflin Company (1997).

Lemann, Nicholas. *The Big Test: The Secret History of the American Meritocracy.* New York: Farrar, Straus and Giroux (1999).

———. "Behind the SAT." *Newsweek* (September 6, 1999): 52–57.

———. "Is There a Cognitive Elite in America?" In Bernie Devlin, et. al., ed. *Intelligence, Genes, & Success: Scientists Respond to The Bell Curve.* New York: Springer-Verlag (1997).

Letts, Quentin, "From mighty acorns, little oaks do grow (a new hereditary elite is springing up)." *New Statesman* 128, no. 4436 (May, 17 1999): 16.

Levy, Frank. *The New Dollars and Dreams: American Incomes and Economic Change.* New York: Russell Sage Foundation (1988).

Lincoln Financial Group. Survey conducted by Roper Starch Worldwide, January 14–January 19, 1999. Retrieved March 15, 2005 from the iPOLL Databank, The Roper Center for Public Opinion Research, University of Connecticut.

Lippmann, Walter. *The Phantom Public.* New Brunswick: Transaction Publishers (1993). Originally published in 1927 by the MacMillan Company.

———. *Public Opinion.* New York: Free Press (1997). Originally published in 1922 by the MacMillan Company.

Lipset, S.M. "Affirmative action and the American creed." *Wilson Quarterly* 16, (Winter 1992): 52–62.

———. *American Exceptionalism: A Double Edged Sword.* New York: W.W. Norton & Company (1996).

———. *Political Man: The Sociological Bases of Politics.* Originally published in 1959. Baltimore: Johns Hopkins University Press (1994).

Locke, John. *Two Treatises of Government*. Edited by Peter Laslett Cambridge, UK: Cambridge University Press (1960).

Lockerbie, Brad, and Stephen A. Borrelli. "Question Wording and Public Support for Contra Aid, 1983–1986." *Public Opinion Quarterly* 54, no. 2 (Summer 1990): 195–208.

Louis Harris & Associates Survey. September 1971. Retrieved March 15, 2005 from the iPOLL Databank, The Roper Center for Public Opinion Research, University of Connecticut.

Louis Harris & Associates Survey. July 13–July 16, 1995. Retrieved March 15, 2005 from the iPOLL Databank, The Roper Center for Public Opinion Research, University of Connecticut.

Lutheran Brotherhood. Survey conducted by Louis Harris & Associates, July 27–August 8, 1993. Retrieved March 15, 2005 from the iPOLL Databank, The Roper Center for Public Opinion Research, University of Connecticut.

Manza, Jeff, and Clem Brooks. "The Gender Gap in U.S. Presidential Elections: When? Why? Implications?" *The American Journal of Sociology* 103, no. 5 (March 1998): 1235–66.

Market Strategies Survey. May 3–May 5, 1999. Retrieved March 15, 2005 from the iPOLL Databank, The Roper Center for Public Opinion Research, University of Connecticut.

McClosky, Herbert, and John Zaller. *The American Ethos: Public Attitudes toward Capitalism and Democracy*. Cambridge: Harvard University Press (1984).

McNamee, Stephen J., and Robert K. Miller. *The Meritocracy Myth*. New York: Rowman & Littlefield (2004).

Meier, August, and Elliot Rudwick. *CORE: A Study in the Civil Rights Movement*. New York: Oxford University Press (1973).

Menchik, Paul L., and Nancy J. Jianakoplos. "Economics of Inheritance." In Robert K. Miller and Stephen J. McNamee (eds.), *Inheritance and Wealth in America*. New York: Plenum Press (1998).

Michels, Robert. *Political Parties: A Sociological Study of the Oligarchical Tendencies of Modern Democracy*. New York: The Free Press (1962).

Mill, John Stuart. *Utilitarianism, Liberty, and Representative Government*. New York: E. P. Dutton and Company (1951).

Miller, David. *Principles of Social Justice*, Cambridge: Harvard University Press (1999).

Miller, Gary. *Managerial Dilemmas: The Political Economy of Hierarchy*. Cambridge (UK): Cambridge University Press (1992).

Miller, Gary, and Dino Falaschetti. "Constraining Rational Choice." In Irwin Morris, Joe Oppenheimer, and Karol Soltan (eds.), *Politics from Anarchy to Democracy: Rational Choice in Political Science*. Stanford: Stanford University Press (2004).

Miller, Robert K. Jr., and Stephan J. McNamee, ed2. *Inheritance and Wealth in America.* New York: Plenum Press (1998).

Miller, Warren E., and Donald E. Stokes. "Party Governement and the Saliency of Congress." *The Public Opinion Quarterly* 26, no. 4 (Winter 1962): 531–46.

Mirowsky, John. "Age and the Sense of Control." *Social Psychology Quarterly* 58, no. 1 (March 1995): 31–43.

Mitchell, Olivia S. "Comments on Alicia Munnell, Annika Sundén, Mauricio Soto, and Catherine Taylor 'The Impact of Defined Contribution Plans on Bequests'." In Alicia H. Munnell and Annika Sundén (eds.), *Death and Dollars: The Role of Gifts and Bequests in America.* Washington, D.C.: Brookings Institution Press (2003).

Morone, James A. *The Democratic Wish: Popular Participation and the Limits of American Government.* Revised edition. New Haven: Yale University Press (1998).

Mosca, Gaetano. *The Ruling Class (Elementi di Scienza Politica).* Trans. Hannah D. Kahn, edited by Arthur Livingston. New York: McGraw-Hill (1939).

Munnell, Alicia H., and Annika Sundén (eds.), *Death and Dollars: The Role of Gifts and Bequests in America.* Washington, D.C.: Brookings Institution Press (2003).

Murray, Charles. *Losing Ground: American Social Policy 1950–1980.* New York: Basic Books (1984).

Murray, Charles and Richard J. Herrnstein. *The Bell Curve: Intelligence and Class Structure in American Life.* New York: Free Press Paperbacks (1994)

National Opinion Research Center (NORC). The University of Chicago, General Social Survey (GSS) 1984, Cumulative GSS data file 1972–2002 [Computer file]. Ann Arbor, MI: Inter-university Consortium for Political and Social Research.

National Opinion Research Center (NORC). The University of Chicago, General Social Survey (GSS) 1991, Cumulative GSS data file 1972–2002 [Computer file]. Ann Arbor, MI: Inter-university Consortium for Political and Social Research.

National Opinion Research Center, University of Chicago Survey. February 6–June 26, 2002. Retrieved March 15, 2005 from the iPOLL Databank, The Roper Center for Public Opinion Research, University of Connecticut.

NBC News Survey. February 21–February 22, 1978. Retrieved March 15, 2005 from the iPOLL Databank, The Roper Center for Public Opinion Research, University of Connecticut.

NBC News and The Wall Street Journal. Survey conducted by Hart and Teeter Research Companies, June 19–June 23, 1997. Retrieved March 15, 2005 from the iPOLL Databank, The Roper Center for Public Opinion Research, University of Connecticut.

NBC News and The Wall Street Journal. Survey conducted by Hart and Teeter Research Companies, December 4–December 8, 1997. Retrieved March 15, 2005 from the iPOLL Databank, The Roper Center for Public Opinion Research, University of Connecticut.

NBC News and The Wall Street Journal. Survey conducted by Hart and Teeter Research Companies, February 26–March 1, 1998. Retrieved February 22, 2005 from the iPOLL Databank, The Roper Center for Public Opinion Research, University of Connecticut.

NBC News and The Wall Street Journal. Survey conducted by Hart and Teeter Research Companies, January 13–January 15, 2000. Retrieved March 15, 2005 from the iPOLL Databank, The Roper Center for Public Opinion Research, University of Connecticut.

Newsweek. Survey conducted by Princeton Survey Research Associates, June 24–June 25, 1999. Retrieved March 15, 2005 from the iPOLL Databank, The Roper Center for Public Opinion Research, University of Connecticut.

Niebuhr, Reinhold. *Moral Man and Immoral Society: A Study in Ethics and Politics*. New York: Touchstone (1995). Originally published in 1932 by Charles Scribner's Sons.

Norrander, Barbara. "The Independence Gap and the Gender Gap" *The Public Opinion Quarterly* 61, no. 3 (Autumn 1997): 464–76.

Noya Miranda, Francisco Javier. "The Value of Ambivalence. Attitudes toward Meritocracy, Equality and the Welfare State in Spain in Comparative Perspective." Original Title "El valor de la ambivalencia. Las actitudes ante la meritocracia, la igualdad y el Estado de Bienestar en Espana en perspectiva comparada." *Revista Espanola de Investigaciones Sociologicas* vol. 86 (April–June 1999): 185–221.

Nozick, Robert. *Anarchy, State, and Utopia*. New York: Basic Books (1974).

Nye, Robert. "The Anti—Democratic Sources of Elite Theory: Pareto, Mosca, and Michels." *SAGE Professional Papers in Contemporary Political Sociology*. Beverly Hills: Sage (1977).

Oller, John. "Monoglottosis: What's Wrong with the Idea of the IQ Meritocracy and Its Racy Cousins?" *Applied Linguistics* 18, no. 4 (December 1997): 467–507.

Orzag, Peter R. "Comments on Pierre Pestieau 'The Role of Gift and Estate Transfers in the United States and Europe.'" In Alicia H. Munnell and Annika Sundén (eds.), *Death and Dollars: The Role of Gifts and Bequests in America*. Washington, D.C.: Brookings Institution Press (2003).

Page, Benjamin I., and Robert Y. Shapiro. *The Rational Public: Fifty Years in Americans' Policy Preferences*. Chicago: University of Chicago Press (1992).

Paine, Thomas. *Common Sense*. New York: Penguin (1976). Originally published by W. and T. Bradford in 1776.

Parsons, Talcott. "The School Class as a Social System: Some of Its Functions in American Society." *Harvard Educational Review* 29, no. 4 (December 1959): 297–318.

———. *The Structure of Social Action.* Glencoe: Free Press (1937).

Pax World Funds and National Head Start Association. Survey conducted by Opinion Research Corporation, August 7–August 10, 2003. Retrieved March 15, 2005 from the iPOLL Databank, The Roper Center for Public Opinion Research, University of Connecticut.

Penn and Schoen Associates Survey. August 26–August 30, 1983. Retrieved March 15, 2005 from the iPOLL Databank, The Roper Center for Public Opinion Research, University of Connecticut.

Pestieau, Pierre. "The Role of Gift and Estate Transfers in the United States and Europe." In Alicia H. Munnell and Annika Sundén (eds.), *Death and Dollars: The Role of Gifts and Bequests in America.* Washington, D.C.: Brookings Institution Press (2003).

Pew Research Center. Survey conducted by Princeton Survey Research Associates, November 5–November 17, 1997. Retrieved March 15, 2005 from the iPOLL Databank, The Roper Center for Public Opinion Research, University of Connecticut.

Pew Research Center. Survey conducted by Princeton Survey Research Associates, November 14–November 18, 1997. Retrieved March 15, 2005 from the iPOLL Databank, The Roper Center for Public Opinion Research, University of Connecticut.

Pew Research Center. Survey conducted by Princeton Survey Research Associates, September 28–October 10, 1999. Retrieved March 15, 2005 from the iPOLL Databank, The Roper Center for Public Opinion Research, University of Connecticut.

Pew Research Center. Survey conducted by Princeton Survey Research Associates, August 24–September 10, 2000. Retrieved February 22, 2005 from the iPOLL Databank, The Roper Center for Public Opinion Research, University of Connecticut.

Pew Research Center. Survey conducted by Princeton Survey Research Associates, July 14–August 5, 2003. Retrieved March 15, 2005 from the iPOLL Databank, The Roper Center for Public Opinion Research, University of Connecticut.

Pew Research Center and Princeton Survey Research Associates Survey. August 24–September 10, 2000. Retrieved November 17, 2005 from the iPOLL Databank, The Roper Center for Public Opinion Research, University of Connecticut. Calculations based on the author's own analysis.

Plato. *The Republic*, 2nd ed. New York: Penguin Classics (1987).

Post-Modernity Project at the University of Virginia. Survey conducted by Center for Survey Research, University of Virginia, January 27–April 14, 1996.

Retrieved February 22, 2005 from the iPOLL Databank, The Roper Center for Public Opinion Research, University of Connecticut.

Public Agenda Foundation Survey. June, 1982. Retrieved February 22, 2005 from the iPOLL Databank, The Roper Center for Public Opinion Research, University of Connecticut.

Public Agenda Foundation Survey. September 3 September 16, 1998. Retrieved February 22, 2005 from the iPOLL Databank, The Roper Center for Public Opinion Research, University of Connecticut.

Public Interest Project. Survey conducted by Greenberg Quinlan Rosner Research, June 17–June 22, 2003. Retrieved March 15, 2005 from the iPOLL Databank, The Roper Center for Public Opinion Research, University of Connecticut.

Public Interest Project. Survey conducted by Greenberg Quinlan Rosner Research, April 5–April 8, 2004. Retrieved February 22, 2005 from the iPOLL Databank, The Roper Center for Public Opinion Research, University of Connecticut.

Rachels, James. *The Elements of Moral Philosophy*, 3rd ed. New York: McGraw-Hill College (1999).

Rae, Douglas, et. al. *Equalities*. Cambridge: Harvard University Press (1981).

Rasinksi, Kenneth A. "The Effect of Question Wording on Public Support for Government Spending." *Public Opinion Quarterly* 53, no. 3 (Autumn 1989): 388–394.

Rawls, John. *A Theory of Justice*, Revised ed. Cambridge: Harvard University Press (1971).

Read, Harlan Eugene. *The Abolition of Inheritance*. New York: MacMillan (1918).

Reader's Digest. Survey conducted by Institute for Social Inquiry/Roper Center, University of Connecticut, August 22–August 29, 1994. Retrieved February 22, 2005 from the iPOLL Databank, The Roper Center for Public Opinion Research, University of Connecticut. Sample consisted of those employed full/part-time.

Reid, T. R. "Britannia Waives Old Social Rules: New Upper Crust Must Achieve Status, Not Inherit It." *The Washington Post* (August 12, 2002), Sec. A, p. 10.

Rhodebeck, Laurie A. "The Politics of Greed? Political Preferences among the Elderly." *The Journal of Politics* 55, no. 2. (May, 1993): 342–364.

Rignano, Eugenio. *The Social Significance of the Inheritance Tax*. Trans. William J. Shultz. New York: Knopf (1924).

Riker, William H. *Liberalism Against Populism*. Prospect Heights, IL: Waveland Press (1988).

Roemer, John E. *Equality of Opportunity*. Cambridge: Harvard University Press (1998).

———. "Equality of Opportunity." In Kenneth Arrow, Samuel Bowles, and Steven Durlauf (eds.), *Meritocracy and Economic Inequality*. Princeton: Princeton University Press (2000).

Roper Organization Survey. January 11–January 25, 1986. Retrieved March 15, 2005 from the iPOLL Databank, The Roper Center for Public Opinion Research, University of Connecticut.

Roper Organization Survey. May 31–June 7, 1986. Retrieved March 15, 2005 from the iPOLL Databank, The Roper Center for Public Opinion Research, University of Connecticut.

Rosenfeld, Michel. *Affirmative Action and Justice: A Philosophical and Constitutional Inquiry*. New Haven: Yale University Press (1991).

Sartori, Giovanni. *The Theory of Democracy Revisited: Part I The Contemporary Debate and Part II The Classical Issues*. Chatham: Chatham House Publishers (1987).

Saunders, Peter. "Might Britain be a meritocracy?" *Sociology* 29 (February 1995): 23–40.

———. "Social mobility in Britain: an empirical evaluation of two competing explanations." *Sociology* 31 (May 1997): 261–88.

Schumpeter, Joseph A. *Capitalism, Socialism, and Democracy*, 2nd ed. New York: Harper and Brothers (1947).

Sears, David O., Colette Van Laar, Mary Carrillo, and Rick Kosterman. "Is It Really Racism?: The Origins of White Americans' Opposition to Race-Targeted Policies." *Public Opinion Quarterly* 61, no. 1 (Spring 1997): 16–53.

Sen, Amartya. "Merit and Justice." In Kenneth Arrow, Samuel Bowles, and Steven Durlauf (eds.) *Meritocracy and Economic Inequality*. Princeton: Princeton University Press (2000).

———. *Development As Freedom*. New York: Anchor Books (1999).

Shervish, Paul G., and John J. Havens. "Gifts and Bequests: Family or Philanthropic Organizations." In Alicia H. Munnell and Annika Sundén (eds.), *Death and Dollars: The Role of Gifts and Bequests in America.* Washington, D.C.: Brookings Institution Press (2003).

Skitka, Linda J., and David A. Houston. "When due process is of no consequence: Moral mandates and presumed defendant guilt or innocence." *Social Justice Research* 14, iss. 3 (September 2001): 305–26.

Sorokin, Pitirim A. *Social and Cultural Mobility*. Glencoe: Free Press (1959)

Squires, Gregory D. *Capital and Communities in Black and White: The Intersection of Race, and Uneven Development*. Albany: State University of New York Press (1994).

Taylor, Ronald N., and Mark Thompson. "Work Value Systems of Young Workers." *The Academy of Management Journal* 19, no. 4. (December 1976): 522–36.

The International Social Justice Project (ISJP). International Social Justice Project 1991 [Computer file]. Ann Arbor, MI: Duane F. Alwin, David M. Klingel, and Merilynn Dielman, University of Michigan, Institute for Social Research, Program in Socio-Environmental Studies [producers], 1993. Ann Arbor, MI: Inter-university Consortium for Political and Social Research.

Tomaskovic-Devey, Donald. "The Gender and Race Composition of Jobs and the Male/Female, White/Black Pay Gaps." *Social Forces* 72, no. 1. (September 1993): 45–76.

Tyler, Tom R. "The Psychology of Leadership Evaluation." In Hans Werner Bierhoff, Ronald L. Cohen, and Jerald Greenberg (eds.), *Justice in Social Relations*. New York: Plenum (1986): 299–316.

Verba, Sidney, Kay Schlozman, and Henry Brady. *Voice and Equality: Civic Voluntarism in American Politics*. Cambridge: Harvard University Press (1995).

Tyler, Tom R. "The Psychology of Leadership Evaluation." In Hans Werner Bierhoff, Ronald L. Cohen, and Jerald Greenberg (eds.), *Justice in Social Relations*. New York: Plenum (1986): 299–316.

UBS. Survey conducted by Gallup Organization, December 1–December 15, 2002. Retrieved March 15, 2005 from the iPOLL Databank, The Roper Center for Public Opinion Research, University of Connecticut.

USA Today and NBC News. Survey conducted by Gordon S. Black Corporation, July 29–August 14, 1990. Retrieved March 15, 2005 from the iPOLL Databank, The Roper Center for Public Opinion Research, University of Connecticut.

USA Today/CNN/Gallup Survey. March 17–19, 1995. Stacie, Julie, "Affirmative Action: The Public Reaction," *USA Today*. (March 24, 1995): A3.

U.S. News & World Report Bozell Worldwide. Survey conducted by KRC Communications/Research, February 6–February 9, 1997. Retrieved March 15, 2005 from the iPOLL Databank, The Roper Center for Public Opinion Research, University of Connecticut.

Walzer, Michael. *Spheres of Justice: A Defense of Pluralism and Equality*. New York: Basic Books (1983).

Walters, Pamela. "Occupational and Labor Market Effects on Secondary and Post-Secondary Education in the United States, 1922–1979" *American Sociological Review* 49, no. 5 (October 1984): 659–71.

Washington Post, Henry J. Kaiser Family Foundation, and Harvard University. Survey conducted by *Washington Post*, March 8–April 22, 2001. Retrieved March 15, 2005 from the iPOLL Databank, The Roper Center for Public Opinion Research, University of Connecticut.

Washington Post, Henry J. Kaiser Family Foundation, and Harvard University Survey. March 29–May 20, 2001. Retrieved November 16, 2005 from the iPOLL Databank, The Roper Center for Public Opinion Research, University of Connecticut.

Weakliem, David L., Julia McQuillan, and Tracy Schauer. "Toward meritocracy? Changing social-class differences in intellectual ability." *Sociology of Education* 68 (October 1995): 271–86.

Weber, Max. *The Theory of Economic and Social Organization.* Edited by Talcott Parsons. New York: Free Press (1947).

———. *The Protestant Ethic and the Spirit of Capitalism.* New York: Routeledge (1992 [1930]).

Weinberg, Ian. The English Public Schools: The Sociology of Elite Education. New York: Atherton Press (1967).

Wilson, William Julius. *The Truly Disadvantaged: The Inner City, The Underclass, and Public Policy.* Chicago: The University of Chicago Press (1987).

Wired and Merrill Lynch. Survey conducted by Luntz Research Companies during September, 1997. Retrieved February 22, 2005 from the iPOLL Databank, The Roper Center for Public Opinion Research, University of Connecticut.

Wirthlin Worldwide Survey. August 6–August 9, 1999. Retrieved March 15, 2005 from the iPOLL Databank, The Roper Center for Public Opinion Research, University of Connecticut.

Wolff, Edward N. "The Impact of Gifts and Bequests on the Distribution of Wealth." In Alicia H. Munnell and Annika Sundén (eds.), *Death and Dollars: The Role of Gifts and Bequests in America.* Washington, D.C.: Brookings Institution Press (2003).

World Values Survey (WVS) 1995, WVS 1981–1984, 1990–1993, and 1995–1997 [Computer file], ICPSR version. Ann Arbor, MI: Ronald Inglehart, et. al., Institute for Social Research [producer], (1999). Ann Arbor, MI: Inter-university Consortium for Political and Social Research [distributor], (2003).

Young, Michael. *The Rise of the Meritocracy.* New Brunswick: Transaction Publishers (1994). Originally published by Thames and Hudson in 1958.

Zaller, John R. *The Nature and Origins of Mass Opinion.* Cambridge, UK: Cambridge University Press (1992).

"Absence of Meritocracy causes breakdown of trust in system: NAB." *The Pakistan Newswire* (March 4, 2005).

"Ever higher society, ever harder to ascend—Meritocracy in America; Meritocracy in America." *Economist* (January 1, 2005), Special Report (2).

"Iranian Government Must Pay Attention to Management, Meritocracy—Former FM." *BBC Monitoring International Reports* (December 7, 2004)

"Meritocracy." *Economist* 324 (Sep. 26 1992): 56.

"Singapore Will Never Compromise Policy of Multiracialism: PM Lee." *Channel NewsAsia* (January 29, 2005).

"Subject Executives to the Merit–Based Pay System." *The Asahi Shimbun* (December 1, 2004).

"The Estate Tax: Myths and Realities." *The Center on Budget and Policy Priorities.* Accessed January 23, 2006: www.cbpp.org/pubs/estatetax.htm.

"The impossible dream? (American intellectuals are losing faith in the merits of meritocracy but have little to replace it; review article)." *Economist* 340 (July 13, 1996): 89–90.

Index